The Classical Guitar

A COMPLETE HISTORY

A BALAFON BOOK

AN IMPRINT OF OUTLINE PRESS LIMITED

THE CLASSICAL GUITAR

A COMPLETE HISTORY
BASED ON THE RUSSELL CLEVELAND COLLECTION

A BACKBEAT BOOK

First edition 2002

Published by Backbeat Books

600 Harrison Street.

San Francisco. CA94107

www.backbeatbooks.com

An imprint of The Music Player Network

United Entertainment Media Inc.

Published for Backbeat Books by Outline Press Ltd.

115J Cleveland Street. London W1T 6PU. England.

www.backbeatuk.com

ISBN 0-87930-725-0

CREATIVE DIRECTOR: NIGEL OSBORNE

DESIGN: SALLY STOCKWELL

GUITAR PHOTOGRAPHY: MIKI SLINGSBY

PRODUCTION: PHIL RICHARDSON

Printed in Hong Kong by Colorprint Offset

02 03 04 05 06 5 4 3 2 1

CONSULTANTS

Paul Fischer provided expert guidance for this book on guitar anatomy and the musical applications of timbers. He is probably England's most experienced classical guitar maker. He worked with guitar-maker David Rubio for six years, and established his own studio in 1975, moving to his present location in Oxfordshire four years later. He has customers in more than 20 countries, including many famous classical guitarists.

Robert Spencer has an immense library of 17th-19th century guitar music, some of which was used to illustrate various sections of this book. He is a lutenist-singer who specialises in Elizabethan/Jacobean song, performing solo programmes and teaching masterclasses. He is a founding member of The Julian Bream Consort, has contributed to scholarly journals such as *Early Music*, and performs throughout the world.

Raymond Ursell helped to make the connections that ensured this book happened. He is a leading dealer in classical guitars. and studied as a professional classical guitarist at the Guildhall School of Music & Drama. He has been buying and selling fine instruments for over 20 years. His international clientle has more recently grown to include a number of rock musicians, such as Sting and his guitarist Dominic Miller.

AUTHORS

Tony Bacon is a leading author on guitar history and a co-founder of Balafon, the foremost publisher of guitar history books. His works include *The Ultimate Guitar Book* and *The Chinery Collection – 150 Years of American Guitars*, as well as various titles in Balafon's popular *Profiles* and *Decades* series.

Colin Cooper is one of the world's most respected writers on the classical guitar. He has since 1982 been features editor of *Classical Guitar* magazine. He is also the author of a number of novels and plays, in addition to his hugely varied writing on the guitar, which includes a regular column in Japan's *Gendai Guitar* magazine. He has judged many international guitar competitions, and is a keen photographer, contributing many artist photographs to music journals around the world.

Jaap van Eik is a journalist who since 1977 has concentrated on writing about music. He is currently editor of the leading Dutch musicians' magazine, *Music Maker*. While still an art student he studied classical guitar for a number of years, later playing bass guitar in various bands in the Netherlands.

Paul Fowles has been writing for the British magazine *Classical Guitar* since 1984. He is also active as a publisher of music for acoustic guitar. Current projects include an early work by Nikita Koshkin and a seven-volume anthology of pieces by Agustín Barrios Mangoré transcribed from the original recordings by Chris Dumigan.

Brian Jeffery has taught at the University of St Andrews. Scotland, and at the University of California, Berkeley. He is the author of the standard biography *Fernando Sor – Composer and Guitarist* and the editor of the standard complete editions of Sor and Giuliani. His interests include medieval and Renaissance literature as well as music.

Richard Johnston founded Gryphon Stringed Instruments with partner Frank Ford in 1969. He is a contributing editor of *Acoustic Guitar* magazine, and co-author of *Martin Guitars, An Illustrated Celebration of America's Premier Guitarmaker*. He is not to be confused with the current editor of *Guitar Player* magazine, who bears the same name but is a different individual entirely.

Tim Miklaucic is the president and CEO of Guitar Salon International, one of the largest dealers of classical and flamenco guitars in the world, and the exclusive US distributor of Ramírez guitars. He has studied classical guitar extensively with Celine, Pepe and Celedonio Romero from 1979 to the present. He also writes for GSI a quarterly *Newsletter* on the classical and flamenco guitar which is distributed worldwide.

John Morrish edited this book, as well as contributing various essays. He is an experienced journalist and author with a special interest in music, and a former editor of the London listings magazine, *Time Out*. He is the editor of Balafon's *Piano*, the first extensively illustrated and detailed history of the instrument. He is also the author of *Magazine Editing*, a textbook for would-be magazine editors.

Heinz Rebellius is a journalist and ex-professional musician. He founded the respected German musicians' magazine *Solo* in 1987 and was editor for a number of years. He also founded *Akustik Gitarre* magazine. He contributes to a number of other publications, including *Fachblatt*, *Frankfurter Allgemeine Zeitung* and *Gitarre & Bass*.

Dr. Bernard Richardson is currently a Lecturer in the Department of Physics and Astronomy at the University of Wales, Cardiff. For the past 20 years he has undertaken scientific research into the acoustics of stringed musical instruments, specialising particularly in guitars. He lectures worldwide on the subject. His research stems from a long-standing passion for making and playing musical instruments.

Dr. Paul Sparks has worked with many of Britain's leading orchestras as a guitarist and mandolinist, and is also a musicologist specialising in the history and repertoire of plucked instruments. He is the author of *The Early Mandolin* and *The Classical Mandolin*, and (together with James Tyler) is currently preparing articles on guitar and mandolin for the forthcoming edition of *The New Grove Dictionary of Music and Musicians*.

Graham Wade is a leading author on the guitar. His many works include *Traditions of the Classical Guitar*, as well as *Segovia – A Celebration of the Man and his Music*, and *Joaquín Rodrigo – Concierto de Aranjuez*. He has played the guitar since 1953 and has given recitals in a number of countries. He contributes to many magazines, and is currently Tutor in Guitar for the Universities of Leeds and York, Chief External Examiner in guitar at the Royal Scottish Academy of Music & Drama, and an Examiner for the Welsh College of Music & Drama.

Brook Zern originally learned flamenco guitar in New York from his Pennsylvania-Dutch father, who had inexplicably become obsessed with the art. Brook subsequently studied flamenco extensively in Seville and environs, and has written about the art for *The New York Times*, *Music Journal* and many other publications. He is the flamenco editor of *Guitar Review*.

CONTENTS

FOREWORD

by RUSSELL CLEVELAND
DALLAS, TEXAS, JULY 1997

In 1955, I was listening to the radio and heard a sound which was so beautiful and mysterious that to this day I still remember the melody. The guitarist turned out to be the great Andrés Segovia, playing *Danza Española no. 10*, by Granados. I was so intrigued with the sound that I found a new love had come into my life: the classical guitar. It remains there to this day.

The classical guitar is one of the few instruments in the world in which the sound is produced directly by hands on strings. The vibration of strings and wood produces a beautiful, almost melancholic sound: that is capable of evoking a variety of different emotions in its listeners.

The guitar is an ancient instrument, and for most of us its music is strongly associated with Spain. Today, however, the guitar is a truly international instrument, being built and played all over the world. There are great makers in Europe, the United States, Latin America, Australia and Japan.

I purchased my first guitar in college, from a gentleman who had unfortunately flunked out of school and needed money to get home. He sold his guitar to me for $20 but as part of the transaction he had to teach me to play. We spent all one evening, until about 3.00 the next morning, trying to learn none other than *Malagueña*. I took lessons for many years, and while I don't consider myself an accomplished player, I enjoy the classical guitar in a way that provides enormous satisfaction.

Some years ago I began looking for a classical guitar that had a beautiful, unique sound. This is the way my collection began. Quite by luck, I bought a guitar in New York City, made in 1912 by the great Spanish builder Manuel Ramírez. It was in that year that Ramírez presented a guitar to Andrés Segovia which the maestro used until 1937, when he switched to an instrument made by Hermann Hauser.

This beautiful old guitar began to fascinate me. I wanted to trace other makers of that era, and became interested in how the classical guitar evolved. What I found was that the great classical guitars were made by artisans, sometimes making only a few instruments in their lifetimes. These instruments were signed, on labels or on the internal wood surfaces, demonstrating the immense pride that went into their making.

As a collector, I found that you could trace generations of guitar builders, such as the Ramírez family, which extends from José Ramírez I, in the 19th century, through to José Ramírez IV today. Or you could trace workers who had, for example, been trained under Manuel Ramírez, such as Domingo Esteso and Santos Hernández.

I found that you could discover rich traditions in different countries and cities. In Paris, for example, there were builders such as J. Gómez Ramírez, who trained Robert Bouchet, and today Daniel Friederich. In Germany, Hermann Hauser began making guitars in the early 1900s, reaching a climax with the famous instrument he made in 1937 for Segovia. His work was carried on by Hermann Hauser II and now Hermann Hauser III. Back in Madrid, the Ramírez family, through workers in their shop, created several generations of new builders.

The story of the classical guitar, beginning with Torres, is not a search for better finishes or more complex decoration but for a more beautiful sound. What I like most about my collection is the fact that all these guitars are playable. Every guitar has a special presence about it that distinguishes the maker.

The classical guitar, while best known for the type of music associated with Andrés Segovia and his successors, has been used in many other types of music. Recently there has been a renaissance in the area of flamenco, following the success of The Gipsy Kings and others. And several players have used the classical guitar to make popular music in a new and intriguing way. I believe we will see a resurgent interest in the instrument, particularly in recording, because of the beautiful sound it can produce.

I have often been asked which is my best sounding guitar. Several times a year, a group of excellent guitarists gathers at my country house to play most of my guitars, but even after a weekend of playing it is difficult to decide which guitar sounds the best. It reminds me of the saying that beauty is in the eye of the beholder.

One guitar that always comes near the top is the José Ramírez "AM" 1969 guitar that was played by Andrés Segovia for many years. Carlo Pezzimenti recently completed his tenth recording, *España*, using this guitar. Those that I love to play personally start with the Vicente Arias 1906, which has a delicate, beautiful sound. And if you've ever played a guitar by Santos Hernández, who was trained in the Manuel Ramírez workshop, you will know why he is considered one of the great makers. My 1933 Santos Hernández classical must be one of the best guitars ever made.

But I could also mention the Hausers, I, II and III. In 1955, Manuel Velázquez made one of the guitars in my collection as a direct copy of a Hauser: he may even have out-Hausered Hauser, as this guitar is not only easy to play but has a gorgeous tone.

My Ramírez guitars date back to 1897, but I particularly love the 1956 José Ramírez II. This is a guitar you could start playing at 6pm one evening and still be playing at 6am the next morning. Another guitar with a real presence about it is the Miguel Rodriguez "church door" guitar, made in 1976 and once played by one of the Romeros.

Other instruments, such as those by Fleta, Friederich, Humphrey and Smallman, are guitars that any concert artist would love to play. And I have several exquisite guitars in workmanship and sound, among them a maple Bernabé, made in 1992, and a José Romanillos made in 1996. Both of these are so exquisite in workmanship that it is hard to imagine anyone building a finer guitar. In skilled hands these guitars are more than just instruments: they are living works of art.

In this book you will meet and learn about most of the great makers of the past 150 years. I have personally met many of today's prominent guitar makers and builders. I can tell you there is a wonderful body of current builders, producing extremely fine guitars.

Some years ago I spoke with Thomas Humphrey, the American guitar maker, and told him that I wanted, no matter what the cost, the most beautiful guitar he had ever made. He said his most beautiful guitar was yet to come, and that every guitar he makes is better than the last. The history of the guitar is one of great beauty, tradition and craftsmanship. I hope Humphrey is right, and that the best classical guitars are yet to be made.

INTRODUCTION

by COLIN COOPER

To make a trumpet, said Mahler, you take a hole and you wrap a piece of tin around it. The guitar's construction is scarcely less simple: you take a hole and you build a wooden box around it. Across that box you stretch some strings, under which you attach a strip of wood so that you can press your fingers against the strings and so alter their pitch.

Of course the process does not end there. Two highly skilled people are needed before your simple box can give out music. One is the player, who must devote years of study to finding out exactly how to activate those strings so that the sounds the box makes are musical sounds. The other is the builder, the luthier, without whose expertise the full potential of the box cannot be realised by the player.

The enthusiasm with which the guitar was taken up in the 1960s and 1970s has resulted in a proliferation of mature talent, both in building and playing. Possibly at no time in history have there been so many excellent instruments in existence, with equally excellent musicians to play them. The only drawback – and it is a serious one in economic terms – is that the guitar's audience has largely deserted it. A concert hall that was full for an indifferent guitarist in 1967 may be, in 1997, only half full to hear a guitarist of acknowledged brilliance.

It is possible that this decline in audience numbers is linked with the gradual trivialisation of music. Music all too easily becomes muzak, a background noise ever present in supermarkets, restaurants and even five-star hotels. We cannot switch it off, but we can at least make no conscious effort to listen to it. That quickly becomes a habit, and a bad one, so that when occasionally a piece by, say, Mozart comes out of the speakers, it merges almost imperceptibly into the mush that precedes and follows it. If someone should happen to notice the good stuff among the trivia, the next step could well be to buy some Mozart and play it at home. But the quantum leap from the hi-fi to the concert hall is something that, given present levels of inertia, seems less and less likely to happen as electronic technology improves.

It is ironic that the very technology that makes it so easy to listen to music at home should be the same as that which, by making it fully audible in a large hall, could in different circumstances be the guitar's economic salvation. Without such amplification, the guitar is best suited to the intimate solo recital in a room containing no more listeners than can hear every nuance and every pianissimo, free from the constant fear of losing the musical narrative through a single inconsiderate cough. We call that a small audience, but the uncomfortable truth is that all audiences for classical music are small. When a John Williams plays to 3000 Londoners, where are the other ten million or so? Even if a Pavarotti sings to 20,000, that is still fewer than two persons in every thousand of the city's population. PR people, always imaginative, call this a 'mass audience'. All that can be accurately said is that Pavarotti's minority audience is bigger than the minority audience of your average virtuoso guitarist.

Some have called for a new Segovia, a new Julian Bream, a new figure with the charisma to attract the general musical public. But behind this lie considerations that are more economic than musical. We are given to understand that the profile of the guitar will be changed, that people will begin to flock to the concert halls once more, and that all will be well with the guitar for another generation or two. Did not Segovia say: "It is the artist that the people follow, not the instrument"?

There is a lot of truth in that statement. Britten did not compose the *Nocturnal* for the guitar; he composed it for Julian Bream. People, by and large, do not go to a guitar recital – if they go at all – in order to hear Britten's *Nocturnal*; they go to hear Julian Bream play the *Nocturnal*. Nevertheless, a comparative lack of charismatic figures and the audiences to hear them are not in themselves indicators of terminal decline. The circle of guitar enthusiasts – and it is a very large circle – who keep the guitar going would in any case contradict you with considerable heat over the question of charisma, pointing to David Russell, Manuel Barrueco, Eliot Fisk, Roberto Aussel and half a dozen other guitarists all capable of holding an informed audience spellbound for a couple of hours. What the critics are perhaps seeking is a guitarist who can hold an *uninformed* audience spellbound. That, though it would help the guitar's public image, can be termed an accident. Accidents do happen, but they cannot be relied upon.

The absence of public charisma is certainly no way to judge the overall health of a musical instrument. Measured by the number of people who buy it and who play it, one would be justified in concluding that the guitar is in a state of rude health. Hundreds of thousands of classical guitars are made and sold every year. Where do they all go? A guitar is not a disposable object; it is not something that you renew every year. The only explanation is that large numbers of people are buying classical guitars – and, though the drop-out rate may be considerable, they surely do not buy them just to hang on the wall.

An estimated two to three million people in Japan alone are believed to play the guitar. They support a monthly magazine of 180 pages. The number of guitarists in China cannot even be guessed at. The Shanghai guitar society alone is reported to have around 2000 members. In Beijing there is outstanding guitar talent, with an enviable record of success in international competitions at the very highest level.

Russia has a vast reservoir of guitar talent that needs only better teaching and better materials. The piano and the violin, with their long traditions, survived the decades of cultural isolation; the modern guitar depended too much on the visit of Andrés Segovia in 1926, since when the message has become somewhat distorted, as in a game of Chinese whispers. That situation is being remedied, though slowly.

In all the Scandinavian countries the guitar enjoys wide popularity. Even Iceland, with a population smaller than that of most cities, has mounted a guitar festival. Central European countries such as Poland, Hungary and the Czech Republic are rich in annual guitar festivals and competitions. Spain and Italy both have a number of important international competitions. Germany is particularly well endowed with guitar activity, and so is France. Some brilliant players have come from the Low Countries. There is a new but promising movement to widen the guitar's scope in Turkey, which has established links with Venezuela and recently held its first-ever competition. There has been rapid progress in South Africa, and there has been a busy guitar scene in Australia and New Zealand for many years. Canada too has a number of world-class players.

Britain has guitar departments in all the main music schools. It also has a network of guitar societies, meeting generally for playing experience but occasionally presenting concerts of high quality. The only monthly classical guitar magazine in English is published in Britain, and is read in 82 countries.

Aided by a general national prosperity, the guitar in the US has established itself on the firmest of footings, exemplified by well-paid teaching posts in the main music colleges and universities and a new generation of gifted, highly trained and internationally successful performers.

In many South American countries, the guitar is virtually a national instrument. A tradition of serious composition has grown up since the pioneering of Villa-Lobos in the early part of the 20th century, and works by such as Piazzolla, Gnattali, Ginastera, Lauro, and Nobre – to say nothing of the ubiquitous Barrios – are worth their place in the repertoire. But access to the classical guitar is limited in many of these countries – the poorer classes in, for instance, Brazil, have little opportunity to study the guitar seriously. Cuba however has a thriving guitar culture, an achievement out of all proportion to the size of the population.

This wide and intense interest throughout much of the world is serviced by a correspondingly large manufacturing industry. Most concert guitarists, for obvious reasons, prefer a hand-built guitar made to suit their personal requirements, but for the huge majority a factory-built instrument is the pragmatic answer. Spain and Japan have been the front runners in this operation in the post-war years, though Japan lost much of its European market when the value of the yen went up. Spain was quick to regain the initiative, and now has a number of factories turning out copious quantities of well-made, good-sounding and playable guitars at varying prices to fit individual pockets. For only £120 it is possible to buy an instrument that will play all the music that a guitar costing £10,000 will play. Guitars are rather like hi-fi installations: the price for the basic equipment is low, but after that more and more is paid for smaller and smaller refinements. To the acute ear and the trained fingers of the professional player, those refinements are worth the extra cost.

Strings have to be replaced at intervals that vary according to one's pocket or one's musical sensitivity. In the US, the large D'Addario company and the long-established Augustine company, the first makers of nylon guitar strings, between them can produce tens of thousands sets of guitar strings every day. When you consider that these are only two out of the many string companies around the world, it is clear that someone is playing a lot of guitars and wearing out a lot of strings.

In 1995 the Associated Board of the Royal Schools of Music in London announced the results of an 18-month enquiry into music-making in Britain. The figures, said to be accurate to within two or three per cent, showed that nearly 12 million adults in Britain (26 per cent of the adult population) claimed to be able to play a musical instrument. No doubt some of them were boasting. The three most favoured instruments, in order of preference, are piano (48 per cent), guitar (29 per cent) and recorder (14 per cent). Children favour the recorder (45 per cent), the electric keyboard (30 per cent) and the piano (18 per cent). From five to 14 years, seven per cent of instrument-playing children play the classical guitar. The figure for adults (over 15 years) is 16 per cent. It would be interesting to see whether these figures are mirrored elsewhere in the world.

In any case, it would be dangerous to draw too many conclusions from this study. We might assume, not unreasonably, that the guitar is favoured by more mature people who have progressed beyond the instant gratification of the electronic keyboard, but the advocates of the keyboard might just as easily argue that the revolution has only just begun.

The guitar's simplicity of structure could well be a factor in its survival. There are movements, as there always have been, to increase the number of strings. It would certainly open up a wider range of music and allow greater justice to be done to some of the music already in the repertoire – that of Bach, for instance. But we have seen what happened to the lute. Its strings increased by a factor of over 200 per cent; it became unwieldy and difficult to keep in tune, and amateurs (the mainstay of any instrument) were only too happy to turn to the new keyboard instruments, which offered quicker results for less effort.

There is general agreement that the guitar has not yet reached perfection. While the great majority of players are content with the six-string instrument, guitars have appeared with seven strings, eight strings, ten strings and, principally for the music of Bach, eleven strings. There is even an ingenious instrument called the Brahms guitar, made by a distinguished luthier so that a distinguished player could play that composer's music with greater effect. But while the focus inevitably remains on the six-string guitar, we should bear in mind that the mysterious and subtle beauty of sound obtainable from those six strings is not a tangible fact, merely an acquired taste. Those of us who have acquired it know that no other sound can be quite like it. It enables us to bear with fortitude our comparative lack of a strong classical repertoire. We do not have a Haydn or a Mozart, but we do have a Sor and a Giuliani, and we are only just discovering how good their best works are.

An unprecedented contribution to the guitar's repertoire has been made in the 20th century. The process of persuading composers to write for the instrument was begun by Segovia, though he drew the line well before Stravinsky. It was left to Julian Bream to net the big fish in the contemporary pond, which he did to such effect that now it can almost be taken for granted that among a serious contemporary composer's output of symphonies, concertos and operas will be at least one work for guitar. A composer need no longer wait for a charismatic figure: the instrument has established itself, and its best exponents are more than equal to the demands that a composer is likely to make of it.

That must surely be the most reassuring fact about the guitar's present position. The instrument has a unique capacity for musical expression, and so long as that expression continues to be valued in our increasingly frenetic society, the guitar will continue to be played and music will continue to be written for it.

instrument he had made for his own use several years earlier. Tárrega played it constantly for 20 years, until its top caved in: it was subsequently repaired by Enrique García. Tárrega was a tremendously influential player with a powerful clique of followers. But his support did little for Torres' financial confidence. In about 1870, he abandoned guitar making, returned to Almería and opened a china shop. Arcas gave up playing the guitar professionally at the same time.

In neither case was the retirement permanent. Arcas returned to performing in 1876, by which time Torres was a year into what his labels call his "second epoch". This time, however, guitar making was a part-time activity. There was the china shop to tend: and the family had even begun to take in lodgers. After the death of his second wife, in 1883, he doubled his productivity, turning out about 12 guitars a year until his death in 1892. These instruments, though, were more basic instruments for local players rather than the great virtuosi he had previously supplied.

By this time his hands were shaking so much that he had to ask a young friend, the local priest Juan Martínez Sirvent, to help him with the more intricate work. He had no choice but to work, with two daughters to support (one only 16 and unmarried) and significant borrowings. He died in November 1892 of "acute intestinal catarrh". Although he had acquired three houses in the latter part of his life, the proceeds from their sale did not even cover his debts. He did, however, receive a generous obituary in the local newspaper.

Numerous innovations have been attributed to Torres over the years, from fan-strutting to the use of mechanical machine heads, but Torres' real genius was to find the most important developments of the day, improve them and bring them together. In doing so he created an instrument of a 'rightness' that has never been seriously questioned.

The most fundamental thing Torres did was to increase the size of the body. Torres' concert guitars, introduced in the early 1850s, have soundboards about 20 per cent larger than those of the concert guitars played by Fernando Sor and Dionisio Aguado a few years earlier. The extra area is in both upper and lower bouts, giving his plantilla the figure-of-eight form we now take for granted. Some claim Torres arrived at this shape geometrically. His descendants, according to Romanillos, claim it was based on the figure of a young woman he saw in Seville. Torres' bridges were another step forward: from about 1857, he used a separate saddle, permitting minute adjustment of string height.

Torres knew that lightness was essential in the vibrating surface of an instrument. But a large soundboard, though potentially louder, is heavier than a small one. Making it thinner to reduce its weight would make it weak and flexible, with unfortunate effects on the sound. The solution lay in building a soundboard that was 'domed', arched in both directions, over an arrangement of wooden struts.

These famous fan-struts would ensure the static strength of the *tapa*, the soundboard, while letting it respond to the vibrations of the strings (see page 8 for a modern soundboard in Torres style).

The system's efficacy was proved by Torres' experimental guitar, built in 1862, with papier-mâché sides and back. This is no longer playable, but those who heard it accepted its maker's contention – confirmed by modern physicists – that only the top of a guitar is of real importance in determining the character of its sound.

Machine heads were not new when Torres used them, in 1856, but they were not common in the Spanish tradition. A more important choice, however, was an aesthetic one. Torres insisted that guitars intended for serious music should have only subtle decoration. Previously the guitar had been both a musical instrument and an item of furniture. Even the vibrating soundboards of 18th and early 19th century guitars were loaded with inlays and marquetry work. With the exception of the elaborately inlaid instrument with which he won his bronze medal in 1858, most of the guitars built by Torres were austere in decoration: it was certainly kept away from the functional parts of the instrument.

Torres does not seem actually to have invented much, except possibly the *tornavoz*. This was a steel cylinder of the same diameter as the soundhole and extending it back into the body, intended to give the guitar added projection. Certainly, 'La Leona' is the earliest surviving guitar by any maker to use the device. He used it often during his first period of guitar making, then abandoned it. His followers took it up, but by the end of World War II it was forgotten.

The effects of Torres' work were immediate and obvious. The new posture recommended by Tárrega, with the left leg raised to support the guitar, depended upon the broader Torres instrument. It gave players the stability they had craved since the days of Dionisio Aguado's tripod, and facilitated more complex music at higher positions. The louder, fuller sound of the Torres guitar permitted a wider range of dynamics and musical expression. Small wonder that the Torres guitar was almost seen as a new instrument. Tárrega wrote no method, but his teachings were faithfully handed on to the next century by his pupil Emilio Pujol (1886-1980). In his introduction to Pujol's *Escuela Razonada de la Guitarra* (Rational Method for the Guitar) the composer Manuel de Falla wrote: "It is a marvellous instrument, as austere as it is rich in sound, and which now powerfully, now gently, takes possession of the soul. It concentrates within itself the essential values of many noble instruments of the past, and has acquired these values as a great inheritance without losing those native qualities which it owes, through its origin, to the people themselves." It is difficult to imagine anyone writing these words if it had not been for Torres. ● JOHN MORRISH

The guitars of Antonio de Torres were, thanks to the patronage of Francisco Tárrega and others, in great demand both during his lifetime and afterwards. They were also tremendously influential over other makers, some of whom may have crossed the line between honourable emulation and dishonest forgery.

Manuel Soto y Solares, a Seville guitar maker who may at one stage have shared a workshop with Torres, sold instruments in the Torres style, although some say they were Torres' rejects. In Madrid, Manuel Ramírez built some guitars with Torres labels, before declaring them his own work. In the inter-war period, excellent makers such as Enrique García and Francisco Simplicio in Barcelona improved their own work by copying original Torres instruments, sometimes with uncanny accuracy. But many Torres instruments were simply counterfeited and passed off as the real thing.

According to the researches of José Romanillos, Torres built about 320 guitars during his lifetime, of which 88 are known to exist. Plenty more could yet emerge, and not all will be authentic.

On one level it doesn't matter. Alice Artzt, the American guitarist, owned this instrument in the 1970s. In a *Guitar* magazine interview in 1984, after a long controversy about its authenticity, she said: "We can't dig Torres out of his grave and dangle the instrument in front

SPECIFICATIONS

Maker and date unknown; no serial number; alerce or Argentinian larch top; mahogany back and sides. Hand-dated label.

OVERALL LENGTH: *38¾ ins (984 mm)*

APPROX WEIGHT: *2⅞ lbs (1.3 kg)*

SCALE LENGTH: *25¾ ins (654 mm)*

STRING SPACING AT NUT: *1¹⁹/₃₂ ins (40 mm)*

SPACING AT SADDLE: *2¼ ins (57 mm)*

NECK WIDTH AT NUT: *2⁵/₃₂ ins (55 mm)*

WIDTH AT 12th FRET: *2¹⁵/₃₂ ins (62 mm)*

NECK DEPTH AT 1st FRET: *²⁷/₃₂ ins (21 mm)*

DEPTH AT 8th FRET: *³¹/₃₂ ins (25 mm)*

BODY WIDTH: *13¹⁵/₁₆ ins (354 mm)*

SIDE DEPTH: *3²⁹/₃₂ ins (99 mm)*

✻ *For information about measurements see page 126.*

▼ **MAKER UNKNOWN**

In the 1850s, at the start of his career as a guitar maker, Torres built a special instrument using fine materials and all his technical innovations. With some reluctance, he sold it to Julián Arcas, his first important customer. Hearing Arcas playing 'La Leona' ('The Lioness'), as Torres called it, persuaded Francisco Tárrega to buy a Torres instrument. The guitar below was accepted as 'La Leona'

until the late 1970s, when its status as a Torres instrument was challenged. José Romanillos, guitar maker and acclaimed biographer of Torres, subsequently identified a different guitar as the "true La Leona". Richard Bruné, guitar maker and dealer, has recently examined this instrument, noting that "the outline is at odds with Torres' style and proportions, and, like the head, it stands out as clumsy and poorly proportioned".

◄ *Alice Artzt (b.1943), the American guitarist, recorded this 1979 record of Tárrega's music on this instrument, which she then owned. "Ever since I was fortunate enough to acquire this instrument," she wrote in a sleevenote, "I have found when using it that I am drawn into a much more romantic style of playing by its very fluid mellow sound." She has since remarked that it is "a wonderful, wonderful instrument".*

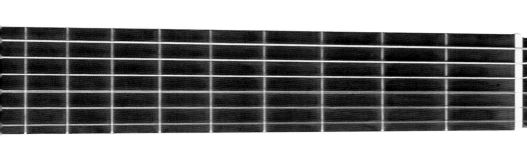

► *Antonio de Torres Jurado (1817-1892), maker of the most celebrated guitars of the 19th century. He left no successors or disciples, which meant there was no one to meet the demand for his instruments after his death. Those attempting to fill the gap ranged from honest imitators, emulating his style, to those seeking to pass off crude fakes as genuine Torres instruments.*

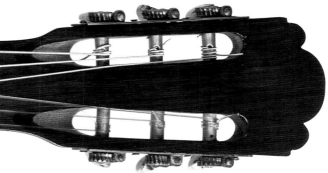

of him and ask him if he made it. I still have no reason to believe that he did not. It's a wonderful instrument."

This is, of course, a musician's argument. There are plenty of others – makers, scholars, collectors, dealers – who will argue that the identity of an instrument is very important indeed, especially now musical instruments are an investment.

Before Artzt acquired it, this guitar belonged to the Otto Winkler collection in the US. In 1966 it appeared in Irving Sloane's *Classic Guitar Construction* alongside four other Torres guitars, its authenticity then unchallenged. In 1978, Artzt played it on a recording of music by Francisco Tárrega (*Guitar Music by Francisco Tárrega*: Meridian 1979). This seemed entirely appropriate for a guitar which she believed, and believes, to be 'La Leona', the first great innovative instrument Torres built.

By this time, however, Artzt had become embroiled in a public argument with José Romanillos, the guitar maker and later biographer of Torres. He was convinced that the guitar was neither 'La Leona' nor built by Torres. The increasingly bad-tempered

dispute raged for several years in the pages of the now defunct British magazine *Guitar* before exhaustion set in. Neither side gave ground.

Eventually, Artzt sold the guitar, via the New York guitar maker Thomas Humphrey, to Russell Cleveland. Cleveland had his collection assessed by the American guitar maker and researcher Richard Bruné, prior to the publication of this book. Bruné proved as damning as Romanillos. He noted that the soundboard was made not of spruce but of alerce, or larch, a wood unknown to Torres. He found the head design and execution, the foot shaping, the fan strutting and much more unlike anything found in known Torres instruments. Most basic of all, he remarked that the shape of the instrument, the *plantilla*, was at odds with what we know of Torres' work. He concluded that the guitar was most likely built in Buenos Aires in around 1930.

Romanillos, meanwhile, has recently restated that he is "110 per cent certain" that the instrument is a fake. In the new edition of his Torres biography he quotes a letter of 1893, describing 'La Leona'. It has few points of similarity with the instrument on this page.

Nonetheless, whatever its age or provenance, this guitar remains an instrument of great musical qualities. ● **JOHN MORRISH**

▲ *These appear to be French machine heads, from the 19th century. 'La Leona' originally had tuning pegs, but many of the guitars of this era have had machine heads fitted, including the guitar identified by José Romanillos as the real 'La Leona'. The label (above left) formed part of Romanillos' arguments against the instrument's authenticity. Printing experts said that some of the typefaces used did not exist before the 20th century. The border bears no close resemblance to any used by Torres and the handwriting is not consistent with that on known Torres labels. But, as Romanillos himself has noted, the label is the least reliable measure of an instrument's authenticity.*

◄ Juan Esteban José Ramírez de Galarreta Planell, better known as José Ramírez I, founder of a dynasty of Spanish guitar makers.

▲ **1897 J.RAMIREZ I**

By the time this guitar was built, José Ramírez I had been an independent guitar maker for about 15 years. Even so, the influence of Francisco González, his maestro, is strong in this guitar. The shape of the head, for instance, is strikingly similar to those on González's large guitars of the 1870s. The large rosette, with its attractive decoration – mother-of-pearl in coloured mastic and wood – is another backward-looking feature. So too is the pointed bridge, found on Ramírez instruments well into the next century. This particular guitar is a small instrument of the type referred to in the Ramírez catalogue as "small size, suitable for senoritas". It was probably not an expensive guitar, being made with cypress back and sides and a spruce top, a combination now seen only in flamenco guitars but then quite often used for the standard instrument. But the presence of a fingerboard and bridge in rosewood, as well as the elaborate decorations, would have made it expensive for a cypress guitar. Even today, this guitar plays and sounds well.

SPECIFICATIONS

Made by Ramírez I in Madrid, Spain, 1897; no serial number; spruce top; Spanish cypress back and sides. Rosette inlaid with engraved mother-of-pearl.

OVERALL LENGTH:	36½ ins (927 mm)
APPROX WEIGHT:	2 lbs (0.9 kg)
SCALE LENGTH:	24⅝ ins (625 mm)
STRING SPACING AT NUT:	1²³⁄₃₂ ins (44 mm)
SPACING AT SADDLE:	2³⁄₁₆ ins (56 mm)
NECK WIDTH AT NUT:	1³¹⁄₃₂ ins (50 mm)
WIDTH AT 12th FRET:	2⁵⁄₁₆ ins (59 mm)
NECK DEPTH AT 1st FRET:	¹³⁄₁₆ ins (21 mm)
DEPTH AT 8th FRET:	²⁷⁄₃₂ ins (21 mm)
BODY WIDTH:	13³⁄₁₆ ins (335 mm)
SIDE DEPTH:	2¹¹⁄₃₂ ins (75 mm)

✣ *For information about measurements see page 126.*

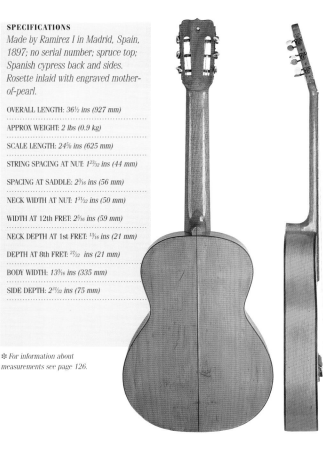

▼ *An interesting early Ramírez label. The address, Concepción Jerónima No. 2, is probably the most famous in classical guitar history. After about a century at that address, the company has only recently vacated the property and found a new showroom nearby. Its workshop, meanwhile, is in the north of the city, where it has returned to its roots in small-scale hand-production. This label, dated 1897 but not signed, also includes a motif featuring two guitars and a bandurria. This is a small Spanish flat-backed instrument, usually with 12 metal strings, played with a plectrum in folk-music groups. Later variants of this label include the words "Construcción de Guitarras Y Bandurrias", making it clear that even the most esteemed guitar makers of the day were also expected to produce a range of other stringed instruments. The Ramírez workshop won a medal at the Logroño regional exhibition of 1887, and an engraving of that, too, found a place on later, more elaborate versions of this label.*

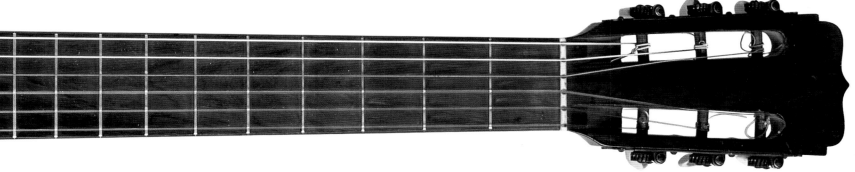

The guitars of José Ramírez I (1858-1923) look backwards: but the workshop he established was to dominate Spanish guitar making to the present day.

Ramírez based his guitars on those of his teacher Francisco González (c.1820-c.1880), and once he had established a style, he stuck to it throughout his life. By the late-19th century, Madrid had developed a strong guitar-making tradition of its own, accepting the fan-strutting and large *plantilla* of Torres but adding a few local idiosyncrasies. Chief among these was the arching of the soundboard, developed by Juan Moreno in the 1830s. The soundboard was arched during construction and held in position by an arched harmonic bar and shaped bridge. The aim was to make the top strong but as thin as possible for efficient transfer of sound.

This was a tremendously influential technique over the next generation of Madrid guitar makers, of whom Francisco González was the most important. He considered himself an innovator, winning prizes at Zaragoza and Paris, and his labels declared that his instruments had "a new and elegant form" and were "built with his own special system", possibly a reference to the arched top.

José Ramírez joined González as an apprentice at the age of 12. He set up in business on his own account in about 1882, taking his famous premises at Concepción Jerónima No. 2 in 1890. There he took on a series of remarkable apprentices: his brother Manuel Ramírez, Enrique García, Julián Gómez Ramírez, who was not a relation, Francisco Simplicio, and his own son, José Ramírez II.

The Ramírez shop must have been doing very well to support such a staff. Its success depended on the Ramírez version of the *tablao* guitar, developed from the large guitars González had made for flamenco players earning a living on the *tablaos*. These were the small stages of the *cafés cantantes*, or flamenco bars, that had come into being in the middle of the century.

Previously an intimate art, flamenco was now a matter of public performance, and the players required instruments that were loud, with a cutting tone. They also liked them new, with the raw edge that comes before guitars are fully 'played in'. Ramírez was happy to oblige, creating an instrument with a large but shallow body in cypress and a domed soundboard. It was still being produced at the time of his death, though many flamencos had by then embraced the smaller, lighter guitars of his estranged brother Manuel.

Not that Ramírez neglected classical players. Although he never built a guitar for Segovia, he was on good terms with Tárrega, who had been so important in the career of Torres. ● JOHN MORRISH

▲ *This instrument has been fitted with typical American machine heads of the late 19th century, minimally decorated, and with the small rollers that are common on instruments of that era.*

of Francisco Tárrega and Isaac Albéniz. Segovia's artistic concepts were thus not only formed at a time when late Romanticism flourished in Spain, but were established well before the collision between the early 20th century avant-garde and the hallowed certainties of traditional culture.

The legacy of Segovia is enormous and complex, in small things as in large. His editions remain an essential part of the repertoire, though many of his arrangements, such as those of pieces by Albéniz, have become less acceptable, giving way to new versions re-worked and brought closer to the original pianoforte score. The patterns of slurs in music by composers such as Frescobaldi and J.S. Bach (including his transcription of the mighty Chaconne in D minor) are no longer in accord with contemporary ideas of performance practice. Yet his example led the way to extended Baroque performance on the guitar. His edition of Twenty Studies for the Guitar by Fernando Sor (1945) has been questioned by scholars, who nowadays prefer facsimile originals, but the book still sells in vast quantities. His recordings from 1927 onwards have nearly all been released on CD.

Segovia's example of performing unamplified in large concert halls is no longer considered the highest ideal. Players now prefer the intimate environment of a small recital room or may use subtle amplification (as does John Williams), to enable the sound of each note to be heard without discomfort. Few players attract capacity audiences internationally in the way Segovia could.

Spanish culture, with all its mystique and romantic allure, has yielded ground to a wide variety of guitar music from many nations. Over recent years Segovia's contemporary repertoire – the music of Moreno Torroba, Turina, Castelnuovo-Tedesco, Tansman and Ponce – has sometimes appeared as somewhat less fashionably popular than the works of Leo Brouwer, Astor Piazzolla or Agustín Barrios Mangoré. Recitals of Renaissance and Baroque music are now played on reproduction lutes, vihuelas and five-course guitars, while for the early 19th century repertoire many performers present 'authentic' recitals on the kind of guitar used by Sor and Giuliani. On the concerto scene, Rodrigo's Concierto de

Aranjuez, never played by Segovia, has been dominant for several years as the epitome of guitar and orchestra. In the conservatoires there are more guitar students than ever, though few concentrate for long on guitarists of the past. Yet each of these developments would scarcely have been possible had it not been for Segovia's massive labours. His presence will always bestride the narrow world of guitar history like a Colossus, through his role in guitar development and the inspiration he gave to players, composers, and luthiers alike.

Our eternal debt to Segovia was expressed by John W. Duarte, writing in Segovia, A Celebration of the Man and his Music, a 90th birthday tribute published in 1983: "Through their works composers may find immortality, in some cases perhaps more prosperously than during their lifetimes; performers survive only through their recordings – and these may in time become unavailable. It is also the way of the world that both may pass through a period of devaluation in which, technical facility having marched on and musical tastes having changed, they are believed to be perhaps less great than they were once considered.

"Andrés Segovia still fills concert halls in the last phase of his incredible career, but he too may eventually have his detractors. When they speak we should, however, never forget that, but for the work and influence of Segovia, there would have been no platform (other than that of salon and coterie dimensions) for us to work on, no global world of the guitar for us to inhabit... We are all standing on his shoulders."

● GRAHAM WADE

● Some images of Andrés Segovia. Left: Segovia's relationship with the Ramírez workshop was extremely important,and was capitalised upon by the company's American distributors in this advertisement. Top: three records from across Segovia's career, showing his range. At left is a Bach recital; in the centre is a collection mainly of miniatures by Spanish and Italian composers; and on the right are his early recordings for HMV of London, including transcriptions and new works written for the guitarist. Often Segovia would disappoint the composers of such pieces by opting to play or record only extracts. Among Segovia's most important achievements was his encouragement of Albert Augustine (1900-1967), the New York guitar maker who developed the nylon string, his portrait appears on Augustine's packaging.

Manuel's apprentice even while he was still working with his brother, built Ramírez-inspired guitars in Barcelona.

As important as these direct connections were the indirect influences. Segovia was so taken with his Manuel Ramírez instrument that he invited other makers to measure and draw it with the hope that they might be able to duplicate its magic. One such scheme led to a permanent estrangement from Santos Hernández, when Segovia had the temerity to praise a Swiss copyist in earshot of the maker of the Spanish original. But it also began Hermann Hauser's career as a maker of Spanish instruments.

Previously Hauser had built excellent guitars in German style, and Segovia heard them played at a concert in 1924 and was impressed. The next day he invited Hauser to measure and draw his 1912 Ramírez, with the aim of producing something similar. By this time Hauser had also seen several Torres guitars, notably one owned by Miguel Llobet, and from then on Hauser's instruments tended to follow either Ramírez or Torres in plantilla, dimensions and internal structure. It took Hauser 13 years to make a guitar acceptable to Segovia, and when he did it was nearer to Torres than Ramírez. Nonetheless, his guitar making in the intervening years had been transformed by the influence of Segovia's Ramírez.

Manuel Ramírez died in 1916, without seeing the international acclaim Segovia would achieve with his instrument. After his death, his journeymen encouraged his widow to keep open his workshop, producing instruments with the label Viuda de Manuel Ramírez. Modesto Borreguero took over, but faded due to what Pohren calls "non-productivity due to bohemianism and irregular working habits".

José Ramírez, meanwhile, lived for a further seven years. His real innovations were not in the realm of guitar making. After establishing his style before the turn of the century he had been content to stick with it. Nonetheless, he is an important figure, not least for his role as a teacher: his brother and son, José Ramírez II, are among his most important students. Furthermore, he was the creator of an important family dynasty, a family firm with great ambitions. He demonstrated this as early as the turn of the century when he was involved in financing and setting up a factory to produce 'student' guitars to be set up and sold in his shop. Initially these "industrial guitars", as José Ramírez III called them, had no labels. Later they were given a plain label distinct from those on the hand-built guitars. In all this, José Ramírez I was a pioneer: throughout its history the Ramírez family has been prepared to think on a larger scale than many of its rivals. ● JOHN MORRISH

► *The elaborate label of Francisco Simplicio, proudly declaring that he is the successor and sole pupil of Enrique García. He also includes a representation of the gold medal that García won at the 1893 Chicago Exhibition. Simplicio was to win a gold medal in his own right at the 1929 Barcelona World's Fair. The label is dated and signed by Simplicio, who took over García's premises.*

SPECIFICATIONS

Made by Simplicio in Barcelona, Spain, 1925; serial number 58; spruce top; Brazilian rosewood back and sides; original French polish.

OVERALL LENGTH: *39⅛ ins (994 mm)*

APPROX WEIGHT: *3 lbs (1.4 kg)*

SCALE LENGTH: *25⅝ ins (651 mm)*

STRING SPACING AT NUT: *1⅝ ins (41 mm)*

SPACING AT SADDLE: *2¹¹⁄₃₂ ins (58 mm)*

NECK WIDTH AT NUT: *1¹⁵⁄₁₆ ins (49 mm)*

WIDTH AT 12th FRET: *2⁵⁄₁₆ ins (59 mm)*

NECK DEPTH AT 1st FRET: *⅞ ins (22 mm)*

DEPTH AT 8th FRET: *¹⁵⁄₁₆ ins (24mm)*

BODY WIDTH: *14¹⁄₁₆ ins (357 mm)*

SIDE DEPTH: *3²¹⁄₃₂ ins (96 mm)*

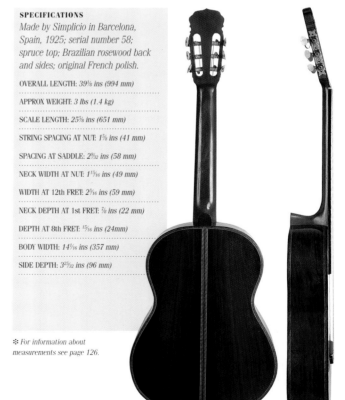

❊ *For information about measurements see page 126.*

There is no doubt that the workshops of José and Manuel Ramírez played a central part in the history of guitar making in Spain. Apprentices trained here would go on to become some of the most important makers of the century.

Enrique García (1868-1922) was the son of one Juan García, a maker of guitars and mandolins. José Ramírez III, custodian of the family's tradition, always insisted that García was trained by his great grandfather, José Ramírez I. José Romanillos, in his biography of Torres, insists that García was apprenticed to Manuel Ramírez. He cites Domingo Prat (1886-1944), who knew García and maintained that he was apprenticed to Manuel Ramírez in his premises at Plaza Santa Ana. Furthermore, as Romanillos has discovered, he is recorded as working there in a census document of 1890.

None of this is of any great consequence. The important event in Enrique García's career was his move to Barcelona, which seems to have taken place in the early 1890s. Barcelona had its own strong, if idiosyncratic, tradition of guitar-making, owing more to French practice than to the Spanish.

Into this potentially hostile environment, García brought the ideas of Manuel Ramírez and Antonio Torres. "His beginnings in this town were difficult," comments René Vannes, in the *Dictionnaire*

▼ 1929 ESTESO
A splendid concert guitar from a maker equally celebrated for his flamenco instruments. Note the elaborate herringbone purflings reflecting the design of the rosette. Esteso's guitars, traditionally braced, have a mellower and softer tone than those of Hernández.

SPECIFICATIONS
Made by Esteso in Madrid, Spain, 1929; no serial number; spruce top; Brazilian rosewood back and sides. The bridge is probably a replacement.

OVERALL LENGTH: *38¾ ins (984 mm)*

APPROX WEIGHT: *3⅜ lbs (1.5 kg)*

SCALE LENGTH: *25⅞ ins (657 mm)*

STRING SPACING AT NUT: *1²³⁄₃₂ ins (44 mm)*

SPACING AT SADDLE: *2⁹⁄₃₂ ins (58 mm)*

NECK WIDTH AT NUT: *2²⁄₃₂ ins (53 mm)*

WIDTH AT 12th FRET: *2⁷⁄₁₆ ins (62 mm)*

NECK DEPTH AT 1st FRET: *²⁹⁄₃₂ ins (23 mm)*

DEPTH AT 8th FRET: *1 ins (25 mm)*

BODY WIDTH: *14¹⁄₁₆ ins (360 mm)*

SIDE DEPTH: *3²⁹⁄₃₂ ins (99 mm)*

✳ *For information about measurements see page 126.*

▲ *The attractively plain and simple label of Domingo Esteso, another celebrated pupil of Manuel Ramírez. Unusually, the label is signed. Esteso established a good trade with South America, and many of his guitars carry a label saying they were built for Romero y Fernández, his representatives in Argentina.*

▲ *The machine heads on the Esteso are German, with engraved sideplates. Once again the lyre motif is in evidence. The oval buttons have a simple elegance. This guitar has been beautifully restored by Paris Banchetti, originally of Uruguay, who now lives in Florida, USA.*

discerning clientele, including flamenco artists such as Ramón Montoya and Niño Ricardo and concert artists such as Regino Sainz de la Maza (1896-1981), dedicatee and first performer of the Rodrigo *Concierto de Aranjuez*. The concert guitars are firmly within the Torres tradition, externally. Inside they often use a downward sloping harmonic bar beneath the soundhole to stiffen the treble side of the soundboard. Hernández's seven fan-struts also tend to run more parallel to the grain of the soundboard than do those of Torres. The object was to improve the guitar's treble response.

The flamenco guitars were designed for strong attack and power, using the standard combination of spruce top and cypress body. Internally, the lower harmonic bar was normally placed straight across the body in traditional fashion rather than being sloped. Hernández's shop became a meeting place for the flamenco players of his day, it was sometimes called "the Parnassus of the guitar".

Despite that, Hernández was a secretive individual who left neither pupils nor heirs. It is said that at any one time he employed only a boy to sweep up. As soon as the boy arrived at an age to show an interest in making guitars he was dismissed. When Santos died, in 1943, his widow took over the shop, employing Marcelo Barbero (1904-1956), who worked for José Ramírez II, to finish the

uncompleted guitars and do repairs. He subsequently became a celebrated maker in his own right. Later he took on Arcángel Fernández as an apprentice, ensuring that some of Hernández's knowledge was passed on to subsequent generations of builders.

Domingo Esteso was born in San Clemente de Cuenca, east of Madrid, in 1882. He joined Manuel Ramírez in the 1890s, staying with him until his death, and then establishing premises of his own at Calle Gravina from 1917. Originally he produced guitars for Ramírez's widow, who in turn supplied them to Romero y Fernández of Buenos Aires, Argentina.

Esteso's concert guitars have no great innovations, but they use high quality materials and have a softer, more mellow tone than those of Hernández. The same characteristic marks his flamenco guitars, which were highly rated by aficionados during his life and have been sought after by collectors ever since. After the death of Domingo Esteso in 1937, his premises were taken over by his three nephews, Faustino, Julian and Mariano Conde, who operated for a while as *Viuda y Sobrinos de Domingo Esteso* [widow and nephews of Domingo Esteso]. Since the death of Esteso's widow in the 1960s they have traded as *Conde Hermanos* [Conde brothers] and today produce a range of factory guitars. ● JOHN MORRISH

▼ **1935 HAUSER I**
A simply beautiful example of the work of one of the leading classical guitar makers of the first half of the 20th century. This is among the earliest models to bear Hauser's distinctive "triple-arch" headstock, and the instrument demonstrates an assured refinement in every detail. While Hauser was clearly influenced by Torres and Manuel Ramírez, he preferred to interpret them through his German sensibility rather than to copy. The maker could ask for no better ambassador than the great Andrés Segovia (right) who used a 1937 Hauser.

◄ *In addition to Segovia, many fine players have been drawn to Hauser I guitars through the years. Julian Bream has played a number, most recently settling on a Hauser instrument made in 1940, and has used the guitar on recordings such as this 1995 CD (left). Brazilian duo Sergio and Eduardo Abreu are seen on this 1969 LP sleeve with a Hauser guitar that was made at around the same time as the 1935 example shown above.*

SPECIFICATIONS

Made by Hauser I in Munich, Germany, 1935; no serial number; European spruce top; Brazilian rosewood back and sides.

OVERALL LENGTH: *38½ ins (978 mm)*

APPROX WEIGHT: *3¼ lbs (1.5 kg)*

SCALE LENGTH: *25¾ ins (654 mm)*

STRING SPACING AT NUT: *1¾ ins (44 mm)*

SPACING AT SADDLE: *2¼ ins (57 mm)*

NECK WIDTH AT NUT: *2 ins (51 mm)*

WIDTH AT 12th FRET: *2⁷⁄₁₆ ins (62 mm)*

NECK DEPTH AT 1st FRET: *¹³⁄₃₂ ins (10 mm)*

DEPTH AT 8th FRET: *³¹⁄₃₂ ins (25 mm)*

BODY WIDTH: *14½ ins (368 mm)*

SIDE DEPTH: *4¹⁄₁₆ ins (103 mm)*

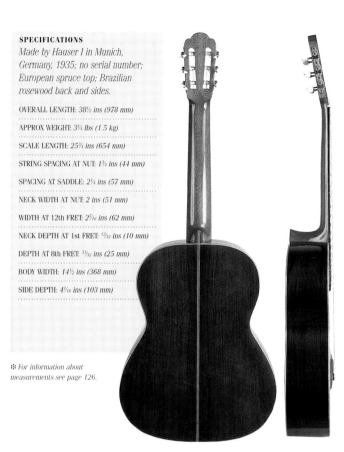

❋ *For information about measurements see page 126.*

▶ *Hermann Hauser, one of the greatest classical guitar-makers, was born in 1882 in Germany, the son of a musical instrument maker. Hermann Hauser died in 1952 at the age of 70.*

◀ *As well as being signed and dated by the luthier under the top (beneath the fingerboard), the instrument also bears this original label signed by Hermann Hauser and hand-dated 1935. In addition, the simple label has printed upon it the maker's workshop address, Müllerstrasse in Munich.*

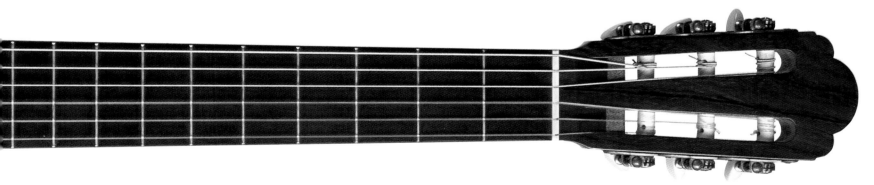

Hermann Hauser is generally considered to have been the greatest classical guitar maker outside Spain, developing the constructional ground-rules and designs laid down by Torres, and applying to them "his Teutonic engineering principles" as Julian Bream once described them. And the wide use of a Hauser guitar by Andrés Segovia certainly did the German luthier's reputation no harm.

Hermann was the son of Joseph Hauser, a maker and player of zithers and other musical instruments, and began himself to make zithers at the age of 18; from 1905 he also built guitars and lutes. (Hermann Hauser is usually referred to as "Hauser I", in order to distinguish him from his son and grandson, both named Hermann, who would also make guitars.) At this time Hauser played in a guitar quartet, and to further this activity he experimented with the construction of alto and bass guitars. However, he attended a concert given by the Spanish guitarist Miguel Llobet, one of the most eminent former students of Francisco Tárrega, during a German tour in 1913-14. Llobet played an 1859 Torres guitar, and Hauser became aware of the possibilities of the Torres tradition. Thus began a process of intense development. According to Franz Jahnel's research, published in his *Manual Of Guitar Technology* in 1981, Hauser had by 1920 reached a number of conclusions after investigating the effects of asymmetrically-arranged strutting. In that year Hauser patented his design for a new type of guitar soundboard. The tops of his guitars were then fitted with one transverse and two longitudinal struts, a transverse strut under the top E-string being intended to strengthen the high-pitched notes.

Hauser first met Andrés Segovia in 1924 during the latter's first concert tour of Germany, and this encounter opened up further possibilities of progress. Segovia, for example, invited the luthier to inspect and measure his famous Manuel Ramírez/Santos Hernández guitar, which the guitarist had acquired from the Ramírez workshop in 1912 before his Madrid debut. Segovia also attended a concert by guitarists playing a selection of Hauser's guitars, as he recalled in a memorial to Hauser I published in *Guitar Review* in 1954.

"The guitars had been constructed by Hauser," Segovia wrote of the concert. "I examined them all and immediately foresaw the potential of this superb artisan, if only his mastery might be applied to the construction of the guitar in the Spanish pattern, as immutably fixed by Torres and Ramírez as the violin had been fixed by Stradivarius and Guarnerius." From this time Hauser worked to create what Segovia would call "the greatest guitar of our epoch". It took him several years, but by 1937 Hauser had produced an

▲ *The headstock of this Hauser I guitar is fitted with machine heads made by Landsdorfer, finished in gold-plate and bearing ivory buttons.*

SPECIFICATIONS

Made by Bouchet in Paris, France, 1961; serial number 81; spruce top; Brazilian rosewood. Refretted and with some revarnishing but otherwise original.

OVERALL LENGTH: 38¾ ins (984 mm)

APPROX WEIGHT: 3½ lbs (1.6 kg)

SCALE LENGTH: 25¾ ins (654 mm)

STRING SPACING AT NUT: 1²³⁄₃₂ ins (44 mm)

SPACING AT SADDLE: 2¼ ins (57 mm)

NECK WIDTH AT NUT: 2³⁄₃₂ ins (53 mm)

WIDTH AT 12th FRET: 2¹⁵⁄₃₂ ins (63 mm)

NECK DEPTH AT 1st FRET: ¹³⁄₁₆ ins (21 mm)

DEPTH AT 8th FRET: ²⁹⁄₃₂ ins (23 mm)

BODY WIDTH: 14½ ins (368 mm)

SIDE DEPTH: 3²³⁄₃₂ ins (96 mm)

✳ *For information about measurements see page 126.*

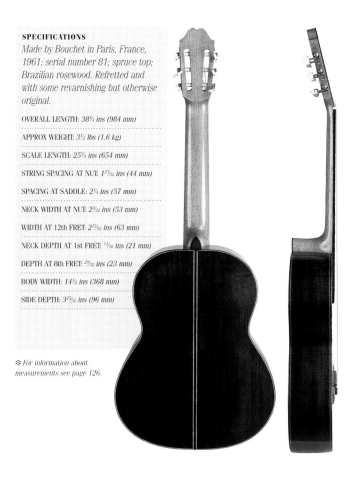

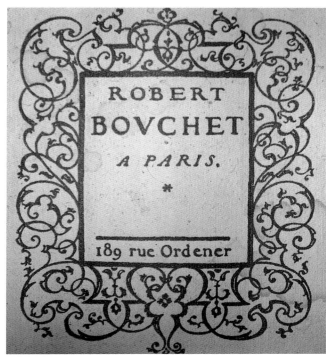

▲ *Bouchet designed and printed his own labels. Early examples, as on the 1946 guitar opposite, have a printed date. But this instrument is signed on the lower transverse bar on the back.*

▼ *Bouchet liked to take responsibility for as much of the guitar-making process as he could. He bought plain machine heads, then silver-plated and engraved them himself in a style reflecting that of his labels. He also carved the buttons. The worm gears are in front of the rollers rather than behind them. This is unusual but not unique. It means that the machine heads will operate in reverse.*

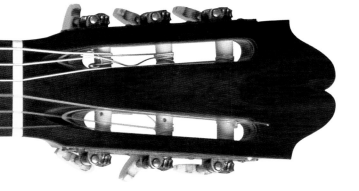

Robert Bouchet (1898-1986) was a painter and art teacher who took up the guitar as a hobby when he moved to Paris in 1932.

As he explained to George Clinton in a 1973 *Guitar* magazine interview, "I couldn't bring my piano with me but I was introduced to the guitar and was captivated at once". In 1938 he obtained an instrument from Julian Gómez Ramírez. "I often used to visit him in his workshop, so that when I came to make one myself, I knew what to do. Actually it was because I lost that nice guitar that I decided to make one."

The loss of that guitar, in 1946, surely changed the course of guitar history. Bouchet's early guitars were modelled on the Torres *plantilla*, and later he adopted the strutting system he had seen in an 1883 Torres guitar he was repairing. In the late 1950s, however, he introduced his own system, with a bar beneath the bridge .

The recordings of Ida Presti and Alexandre Lagoya demonstrate the greatness of his finest instruments. Julian Bream also played Bouchet, commenting to Tony Palmer in the 1982 book *Julian Bream, A Life on the Road*, "He made three instruments for me, the second one being an absolute pearl.

"It had a beautiful sound, and a sustaining quality throughout its whole register rather like a small eighteenth-century organ. I treasured this instrument like no other, until in mid-December 1962 it was stolen from my car."

Bouchet guitars of 1957 and 1962 can be heard on Bream's *Popular Classics for Spanish Guitar* (RCA, 1964). Other owners included Emilio Pujol, Oscar Ghiglia of Italy and Manuel López Ramos of Mexico. A particularly fine example of the Bouchet tone qualities can be found on Turibio Santos's recording of the complete Villa-Lobos *Twelve Studies* (Erato,1968), played on a 1968 guitar.

In 1976 Antonio Marin Montero (b.1933), one of the finest luthiers of Granada, became aware of Bouchet's guitars, and the two makers began collaborating on a guitar. Bouchet, the older maestro, decided on the *plantilla*, its inner construction, the wood for the top and the measurements. Both men were pleased with the instrument.

In 1979, Marin Montero visited France for two months (where he worked with Bouchet on four more guitars), and the following year he began to market the new Marin/Bouchet guitars, with great success. A splendid example, made in 1981, can be heard on the debut recording of the young Russian/Australian virtuoso, Slava Grigoryan, *Spirit of Spain*, (Sony, 1995).

Bouchet's work has been immensely influential in Spain as well as throughout northern Europe. ● **GRAHAM WADE**

1965

SPECIFICATIONS

Made by Oribe in Inglewood, CA, US, 1965; number 069; spruce top; Brazilian rosewood back and sides. Replacement bridge saddle.

OVERALL LENGTH: *39¼ ins (997 mm)*

APPROX WEIGHT: *3½ lbs (1.6 kg)*

SCALE LENGTH: *26 ins (660 mm)*

STRING SPACING AT NUT: *1²³⁄₃₂ ins (44 mm)*

SPACING AT SADDLE: *2¼ ins (57 mm)*

NECK WIDTH AT NUT: *2½₂ ins (52 mm)*

WIDTH AT 12th FRET: *2¹³⁄₃₂ ins (61 mm)*

NECK DEPTH AT 1st FRET: *²⁷⁄₃₂ ins (21 mm)*

DEPTH AT 8th FRET: *²⁹⁄₃₂ ins (23 mm)*

BODY WIDTH: *14¾ ins (375 mm)*

SIDE DEPTH: *3²⁵⁄₃₂ ins (99 mm)*

✽ *For information about measurements see page 126.*

José Oribe (b.1932) grew up in Marion Heights, Pennsylvania, US. As a child he suffered from a bone disease that kept him in hospital for many years. Despite his Spanish heritage, he knew nothing of the classical guitar until he was 23 and a machinist in the aerospace industry in Inglewood, California, when he first heard the instrument played in front of him. He still recalls his eyes welling with tears at the beautiful sound, and considers that the turning point in his life.

He then began an intensive study of the classical guitar, playing at every possible moment. One of his instructors suggested he travel to Spain. Although he did not feel at home in the country his father had left 40 years earlier, Oribe returned to the United States determined to make a career that involved the Spanish guitar.

After a few years of selling guitars, Oribe began building his own instruments in his garage in 1962, later moving the operation to a small storefront. This was a typical classical guitar shop, with lessons and sales of instruments and accessories helping to support the guitar maker in the back room as he struggled to establish a reputation. The guitar pictured here is from 1965, barely three years after Oribe had started. Its highly refined workmanship is an indication of how quickly he learned, something he attributes to being born with "an overabundance of common sense".

▼ 1965 ORIBE

An excellent concert guitar built by José Oribe in 1965. Compared to most Spanish-built instruments, this is a large guitar, wider in the lower bout even than those of José Ramírez III. Oribe's objective has always been to achieve balance and volume in a concert-hall setting, while using a design that remains within the mainstream tradition. This instrument has a spruce top and a Brazilian rosewood back and sides.

Oribe's stocks of rosewood, built up during the 1960s, mean that he can continue to offer the wood despite the ban on exporting it from Brazil. But increasingly he produces guitars made in Cocobolo rosewood (Dalbergia Retusa) from Mexico and Central America. The finish on this guitar is in near-perfect condition even after 30 years. Today Oribe uses French polished shellac on his soundboards but offers a choice of varnish or lacquer elsewhere.

◀ The machine heads on the 1965 Oribe are gold Landsdorfers with mother-of-pearl buttons. The head design is distinctively ornate, and is used to this day. The quality of the woodworking is high, and the finish is exceptional, even after 30 years of use. Oribe works meticulously in pristine conditions to achieve such results. His records of those who have owned or played his guitars include Angel and Pepe Romero, Sabicas, Earl Klugh and Chet Atkins.

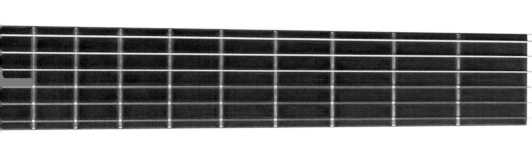

◀ The label of the 1965 Oribe guitar, signed and dated by the maker, showing that it was made in his original shop in Inglewood, California, where he had worked as a machinist in the aerospace industry. Oribe's taste in design tends towards the florid, in the most literal sense. That is reflected not only in his labels but in his head shape and especially his rosettes. His most popular current designs are based on roses and geraniums. He has recently started using a computer program to speed the process of creating a new rosette. This will enable him to change designs more frequently, although each rosette will still require some 17,000 pieces of wood.

José Oribe's ten years as a machinist in a factory environment gave him a distinct advantage: he understood the advantages of efficient production, and the necessity of accurate machining. From the beginning, he stockpiled vast quantities of wood, to ensure proper seasoning, and strictly regulated the climate of his workshop. To this day he focuses on order and control. The Oribe workrooms are as clean as a modern business office and woodchips, sawdust and shavings are instantly removed.

José Oribe and his wife Juanita moved south from Inglewood to Vista, California, in 1973. Here, unlike in their earlier shop, they can dedicate their time to guitar building with little chance of unscheduled interruptions. Their spacious living quarters, largely decorated with guitar-related art and photographs by Oribe, are just steps away from a remarkable production facility in which only two people perform every conceivable task in building a classical guitar. The vast quantities of wood and guitars in various stages of completion suggest a small factory producing hundreds of guitars per year, but the reality is that many parts of an Oribe guitar are prepared years in advance. The meticulous curing of woods between every machining operation, plus careful design, is what has given these guitars their reputation for stability and longevity. Oribe has kept thorough records of his experiments over the years with virtually every aspect of the classical guitar.

Oribe controls every aspect of his craft – he not only designs and builds the rosettes, but dyes the veneers to his own colour schemes. This obsession with control continues to the marketing of the guitars as well, with a newsletter and advertisements prepared in the Vista shop. Most sales are direct to the guitarist, and Oribe instruments are shipped all over the globe. Total production to date is approximately 1500 guitars.

Oribe offers customers many variants on the basic pattern. Three scale lengths, several rosettes and a startling choice of woods again suggest a much larger operation. Though the early example shown here is of Brazilian rosewood and spruce, he has used cedar and also redwood for tops. Cocabolo is Oribe's choice for replacing Brazilian rosewood, and guitars are built with bird's-eye maple on request. José uses a modified Torres bracing pattern, with an angled lower harmonic bar and assymetrical 'V' braces below the fan pattern. ● **RICHARD JOHNSTON**

▲ José Oribe (top) with his wife Juanita and son John Martin Oribe, who has recently started producing his own line of concert guitars from his father's workshop in Vista, California.

1966

David Rubio, who was born in 1934, originally planned a career in medicine but became fascinated by flamenco. He took lessons from Pepe Martínez (1923-1985), the flamenco maestro from Seville, and became interested in guitar making, observing the luthiers at work at close range.

"I went to Spain to study with Pepe Martínez," he told George Clinton in a 1972 *Guitar* magazine interview. "I stayed there quite a while, met guitar makers, got involved in the workshop of Miguel Obando, and then went to Madrid and got even more involved in the Esteso workshop.

"There I pirated: I was a player, so they had no cause to fear me... I was one of those who practised very close to Costino Conde's workbench – for about two years."

In 1961 he moved to New York, attending night school and working for an Argentinian cabinet-maker before establishing his first guitar workshop in Greenwich Village in 1963. A few months later, Julian Bream took a Bouchet guitar to him for repair, and suggested he make a copy of the instrument. The results were very successful and Bream and Rubio became close friends.

A guitar made by Rubio in 1965 was used on Bream's 1966 *20th Century Guitar*, including the first recording of Britten's *Nocturnal*.

SPECIFICATIONS
Made by Rubio in New York, USA, 1966; signed and dated by maker; European spruce top; Brazilian rosewood back and sides; rosewood and ivory bridge.

OVERALL LENGTH: *39⅝ ins (1006 mm)*

APPROX WEIGHT: *3⅝ lbs (1.6 kg)*

SCALE LENGTH: *26⅛ ins (664 mm)*

STRING SPACING AT NUT: *1²³⁄₃₂ ins (44 mm)*

SPACING AT SADDLE: *2¹¹⁄₃₂ ins (59 mm)*

NECK WIDTH AT NUT *2 ins (51 mm)*

WIDTH AT 12th FRET: *2¹³⁄₃₂ ins (63 mm)*

NECK DEPTH AT 1st FRET: *¹³⁄₁₆ ins (21 mm)*

DEPTH AT 8th FRET: *¹⁵⁄₁₆ ins (24 mm)*

BODY WIDTH: *14¹³⁄₃₂ ins (371 mm)*

SIDE DEPTH: *3¹³⁄₁₆ ins (97 mm)*

❋ *For information about measurements see page 126.*

SEGOVIA AND THE GUITAR MAKERS

The life of Andrés Segovia was gradually transformed over many years into a kind of romantic legend. The acquisition of his first guitar from the workshop of Manuel Ramírez became a special part of that legend after 1949 when Segovia wrote about it in the autobiographical episodes he was writing for the New York-based magazine, *Guitar Review*.

Segovia had visited Ramírez shortly before the guitarist's debut in Madrid in 1912. His intention was to hire a guitar, in much the same way as one might hire a piano. Ramírez showed him an instrument that had originally been made in the workshop by the foreman, Santos Hernández, for a blind guitarist named Giménez Manjón.

"I looked at it for a long time before awakening its resonances. The grace of its curves, the old gold of its fine-grained pine top, the delicately worked ornamentation around the exactly placed soundhole; the neck stemming straight and slim from the austere bust with its back and sides of *palosanto,* and ending in a small and dainty head; in short, all of its features, all the lines and highlights of its graceful body, penetrated my heart as deeply as the features of a woman, who, predestined by heaven, suddenly appears before a man to become his beloved companion... I realized that this guitar was the perfect tool with which to fulfil my artistic destiny," Segovia wrote in *Guitar Review* with his characteristic extravagance.

Ramírez's response was to give the guitar to the young artist. Segovia quotes him thus: "The guitar is yours, young man .... Take it with you through the world, and may your labors make it fruitful... For the rest don't worry... Pay me without money.' I put my arms out to embrace him, my eyes full of tears. 'This is one of those acts that have value and no price,' I said, but with a voice so choked and broken that my words could scarcely be heard."

There seems to be no earlier account of this incident in Segovia's interviews and discussions with various writers before 1949. But by that time the Ramírez/Hernández guitar had run its course, having been played for a quarter of a century. It can be heard on the early recordings from 1927 onwards. In 1924 Segovia met the German luthier, Hermann Hauser, who was then producing instruments in the baroque German tradition. Segovia allowed him to take measurements of the Ramírez/Hernández guitar. In 1937 Segovia received from him a guitar which he used for a further 25 years, calling it "the greatest guitar of our epoch".

In 1952 José Ramírez III (great-nephew of Manuel), then still an apprentice, met Segovia for the first time and was instructed in the virtues of the Hauser guitar. Some years later

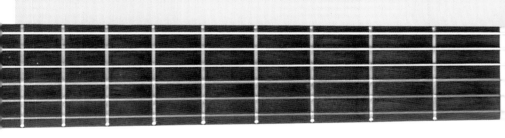

● *Andrés Segovia is pictured (above) with one of a number of Ramírez instruments that he played from the early 1960s. As well as the 1969 instrument pictured on these pages, Segovia also played a 1965 Ramírez III, the soundhole of which is pictured (inset). A document signed by Ramírez III verifying the guitar as one played by Segovia has been pasted below the label.*

Segovia asked José to repair the famous Hauser instrument. The luthier researched and experimented, eventually producing a guitar acceptable to Segovia, who played it on his concert tours of Australia in 1961.

This was the beginning of a long association between the younger branch of the Ramírez family and Segovia. According to Ramírez's account in the 1993 *Things About The Guitar*, Segovia played a variety of Ramírez guitars from this time on, often exchanging them with the maker after a season and taking a new one.

In 1955 Ignacio Fleta (1897-1977), after many years building various other kinds of instruments including vihuelas and lutes, heard Segovia for the first time and decided, according to Siegfried Hogenmüller's obituary in *Guitar* magazine in 1978, to dedicate himself to guitar making. "I heard Segovia playing," Fleta said. "There I decided to build guitars and only good guitars."

Segovia played various Ramírez guitars over the years, despite complaining constantly about the wolf notes (a characteristic of most stringed instruments, where some notes, particularly in the treble, are weaker and less sonorous than others). A severe rift between artist and luthier was maintained for some eight years when, in 1974, Segovia advertised a recital as being played on a Fleta, but performed on a Ramírez guitar.

Segovia performed on Ramírez guitars up to his death in 1987. By that time the instruments of José Ramírez were not the automatic first choice of most top players as they had been at one time. The focus gradually shifted elsewhere as guitar makers proliferated around the globe. The Spanish traditions remained potent, but gradually luthiers of other countries investigated for themselves the central problems, pragmatically evolving their individual solutions. Non-Spanish makers gained international renown, though their guitars are often quite different in design and appearance from the few favoured by Segovia over his long career ● GRAHAM WADE

▶ *José Ramírez III (1922-1995) was the son of José II, and took over the running of the family's guitar-making workshop upon his father's death in 1957. From that time onward he became responsible not only for the production of Ramírez guitars, but as a consequence established many of the attributes of the modern classical guitar, ensuring that it became a more effective concert-hall instrument. He is especially remembered for popularising the use of western red cedar as an effective replacement for European spruce for guitar tops.*

▶ *The headstock of this Ramírez III instrument is fitted with gold-plated machine heads made by Fustero. The Ramírez III guitar at the top of the opposite page has had its original Fusteros replaced with a set of tuners made by Landsdorfer.*

WOOD AND THE GUITAR MAKER

The selection and use of wood is fundamental to the guitar maker's craft. But modern makers are having to come to terms with the fact that the supply of materials is finite and, in some cases, already dwindling.

Consequently, attention has turned to new sources, and new species. An innovator in this respect, as in so many others, was José Ramírez III, who pioneered the use of a wood called western red cedar for soundboards. He was responding to doubts about the supply and quality of European spruce, the long-term favourite in this role. The 'cedar' that Ramírez adopted was, as he was quick to point out, not a cedar at all but a North American conifer called *thuya plicata*. The usable part of the trunk grows up to 20m in height, and each tree produces large quantities of wood.

European spruce wood, on the other hand, comes from a dwindling number of very old trees, and only the comparatively short section up to the lowest branches can be used. Often called German spruce, *picea abies* does not usually come from Germany: more often it comes from the former Yugoslavia, and in recent years the wars raging there have made supply erratic in the extreme.

The lead taken by Ramírez was followed by many makers, including both traditionalists such as Fleta and innovators like Daniel Friederich. But western red cedar has always been a controversial wood. Some makers will not use it at all. José Romanillos, for instance, told Colin Cooper in 1991, "The sound of western red cedar lacks the refinement that in my view is essential to produce a great guitar: a second-rate wood that does not endear itself to me."

Nonetheless, it has acquired a following of its own, although descriptions of the character of its sound vary wildly. Some say it is "mellow" or "sweet", others that it is "bright and clear but less yielding than spruce: it has a will of its own, whereas with spruce the player can bend the sound to what he wants". One thing that is agreed is that western red cedar, unlike spruce, needs no 'playing in'. There are other spruces: Englemann or Sittka spruce is popular in the US, Hokkaido spruce in Japan.

● *Both ends of the process: guitar maker Paul Fischer in his wood store.*

might have come near to it with some very old furniture... Well, one day I sent one of my young fellows to buy wood and when he returned he said the supplier had what he thought was Honduras cedar. I told him to go back and bring a sample. When he returned I saw immediatley that the wood had the characteristics I had always been looking for. I went myself and bought a large piece of trunk, took it to the workshop, and cut a top from it. I gave it to one of my craftsmen and told him to build a top from it. When the guitar was finished we realised at once that although this wood required a different working, it was not only good but superior. At first I was criticised for using it, but little by little more makers realised its worth and changed to it."

This use of cedar was one of the most important and significant developments in the history of the modern guitar. If anyone doubts this, consider that this wood has become the preferred soundboard material for the instruments of the majority of guitar-playing concert artists, including Pepe Romero, John Williams, Christopher Parkening and Manuel Baruecco, to name a few. It also became the preferred wood for tops among several of the world's most acclaimed luthiers, such as Ignacio Fleta, Daniel Friederich and Miguel Rodríguez Jr. Another remarkable and central innovation

occurred in the 1960s when, most probably at the request or influence of Andrés Segovia, José III began to introduce the long string length of 664 mm in his guitars. This gave the instruments more power to project in a large concert hall – and also accommodated the huge hands of the maestro. Although it has in recent years fallen out of favour, this increased string length became the standard among guitar makers and guitarists throughout the 1960s and 1970s, and is still preferred today by many performers who need to fill large concert halls, or those who are lucky enough to find themselves playing with an orchestra.

José III did not, of course, arrive at his designs through chance, and has experimented widely. "I've tried everything," he told Clinton. "Double top; double back; I know all about Lacôte and his experiments with double tops.... Look inside the guitar! We are just doing what 90 per cent of guitar makers have done before. Everybody has a look at the secrets." He also realised early in his career that some people appeared to miss what seems self-evident: the primary aim should be to achieve a fine-sounding instrument. "When I couldn't achieve this I was very upset, and then I determined to study the guitar hard. I soon realised that the guitar was a very detailed work and that I needed more knowledge about

In all cases, planks to form soundboards are 'quarter-sawn', meaning cut from the bark into the centre of the tree, at 90 degrees to the annular rings in the wood. This produces boards which are flexible laterally but strong longitudinally. The soundboards are acquired by most makers as paired, book-matched boards to be joined and shaped. Even at that stage they have their own character.

Hold a piece of spruce in one corner and tap it lightly and it will produce a note: this musical quality can persist through cutting, shaping and strutting, which has given makers great scope for mystification. Some claim to tune their soundboards to a specific note by scraping the wood: b-flat being a favourite. Others say that they tune fronts and backs a semi-tone apart.

On the other hand, many makers doubt that the chosen 'note' survives the assembly and finishing process. Others struggle to suppress any obvious resonances in the hope of producing an even tonal response. The idea, has however, received some support from the scientists: Dr Bernard Richardson at Cardiff University says makers may feel that tuning to a note offers a way to standardise a series of soundboards. Other makers, notably Daniel Friederich, subject their soundboard woods to a battery of scientific tests before beginning the making process.

Since Torres built a guitar with a papier-mâché back, most makers have been agreed that the body of the guitar is less important in determining the quality of sound than the soundboard. Only in our own era has it become an issue again, with makers trying to increase the back's rigidity to prevent it absorbing the vibrating energy of the string or transmitting it into the player's body. Through most of the history of the

guitar, however, the back and sides have been an opportunity to use fine woods for aesthetic purposes.

Torres built guitars in Spanish cypress, a softwood now mainly used for flamenco guitars, maple, mahogany, walnut and something called locust-wood. But the most popular guitar-making wood has always been Brazilian rosewood (*dalbergia nigra*), sometimes called jacaranda, a dark red, rose-scented hardwood from a tropical evergreen tree first imported to Spain within a few years of the discovery of the American continent. In recent years, this has been supplemented by East Indian rosewood (*dalbergia latifolia*). Both are handsome woods. The Brazilian is generally perceived as more beautiful, but it is also more brittle and

difficult to work. The Indian tends to have less impressive figurations, but it grows on plantations and so is available.

Since 1992, an international treaty has banned the export of Brazilian rosewood, an endangered rain-forest tree, from its homeland. Those who use it now must have a licence from their governments to prove that the wood was bought before the ban. And those who own Brazilian rosewood instruments will find it potentially difficult to move them across frontiers: one American maker supplies his customers with a copy of his licence.

Any wood currently being used by a reputable maker is likely to be old, of course, since instrument woods are aged for many years before use. The problems will come in the future. Mahogany, a popular choice for guitar necks, is likely to be banned under the same Convention on International Trade and Endangered Species that placed the restrictions on Brazilian rosewood. More may follow.

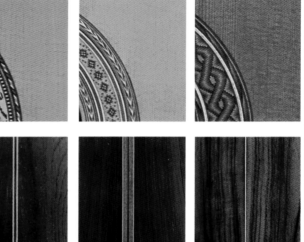

In 1983, Paul Fischer (pictured left), a British guitar maker who had worked with David Rubio, went to Brazil to investigate the supply of Brazilian rosewood and to look into alternatives. On his return to Britain, he built seven guitars using the woods he had encountered there, including Santos Palisander, Princewood and Kingwood, another type of rosewood. A panel of experts voted on the instruments as they were played by the guitarist John Mills. The Santos Palisander was the winner, but all were considered good instruments. Sadly, none of the woods has met with a great deal of demand from players, and Fischer continues to make most of his guitars in Brazilian rosewood. What is more, many of the 'new woods' Fischer investigated have since become rather scarce. ● JOHN MORRISH

● *Some of the more important woods used in guitar making. The top line shows soundboards, where quality of sound is the prime consideration. Makers prize wood from mature trees, with close, straight grain. Left to right: European spruce; Hokkaido spruce; western red cedar; western red cedar in a matt finish. The bottom line shows backs, where cosmetic factors are more relevant. Left to right: cypress; Brazilian rosewood; Brazilian rosewood; Indian rosewood.*

the physics and the science. There might be a little art in making the rosette and putting the guitar together, but the sound is purely a product of physics. I know I'm not doing myself any favours in saying this, because I would like to be thought of as an artist. But it is so."

José Ramírez III was born in Buenos Aires, Argentina, in 1922. His father José II had left Spain for a brief tour of South America after the turn of the century... and ended up staying for nearly 20 years. In 1923, on the news of the death of his own father, José II moved the family back to Madrid, and it was at this time that he took over his late father's guitar workshop. At the age of 18, José III began working as an apprentice and within a few years was building guitars and experimenting on his own. In 1957, he took over the duties as "maestro" (master) of the Ramírez workshop, which by now had spanned three generations, and he continued to develop what would become the Ramírez concert guitar that we know today. This instrument was typified by its large body, long string length, and cedar or spruce top. It had great power, as well as sustain, sweetness, a fullness of tone and a balance across the entire register. José III died in 1995 at the age of 73.

Probably his most enduring contribution will be his role as a teacher and as a developer of talent. We often measure a man's

greatness not only by what he achieves in his lifetime, but by what he leaves behind for others to complete, and by how he influences those in his wake. From the 1960s to the 1990s, the José Ramírez workshop has assembled and trained many of the most talented *guitarerros* of José III's generation, many of whom continue to work on their own with great individual success. This collection of greatness under one roof has only been approached by that of Manuel Ramírez (José III's great-uncle) or his grandfather, José Ramírez I, whose workshops collectively included the likes of Santos Hernández, Enrique Garcia, Domingo Esteso, Emilio Pasqual Viudes, Modesto Borregero, Julian Gomez Ramírez and many others.

José III's roster, however, is still unmatched when you consider the number of great luthiers who began their careers there. They include Paulino Bernabé, Manuel Contreras, Mariano Tezanos, Enrique Borreguero Marcos, Pedro Contreras Valbuena, Manuel González Contreras, Miguel Malo Martínez and so on.

Finally, although there has been much said about José III over the years, it cannot be denied that the guitar which he designed in the early 1960s still stands as the world standard of the concert classical guitar, a standard by which all other guitars are measured and will be measured in years to come. ● TIM MIKLAUCIC

SPECIFICATIONS

Made by Rodríguez in Cordóba, Spain, 1976; western red cedar top; "church door" Brazilian rosewood back and sides.

OVERALL LENGTH: *39½ ins (1003 mm)*

APPROX WEIGHT: *3½ lbs (1.6 kg)*

SCALE LENGTH: *26¼ ins (667 mm)*

STRING SPACING AT NUT: *1¾ ins (44 mm)*

SPACING AT SADDLE: *2⅜ ins (60 mm)*

NECK WIDTH AT NUT: *2 5/32 ins (55 mm)*

WIDTH AT 12th FRET: *2½ ins (63 mm)*

NECK DEPTH AT 1st FRET: *29/32 ins (23 mm)*

DEPTH AT 8th FRET: *31/32 ins (25 mm)*

BODY WIDTH: *14 11/16 ins (373 mm)*

SIDE DEPTH: *4¼ ins (108 mm)*

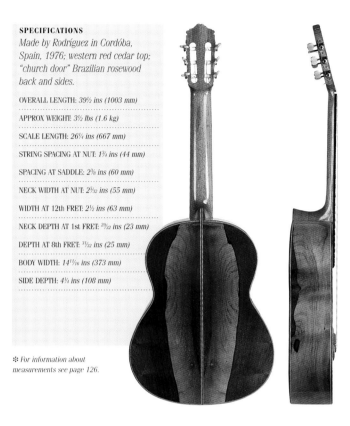

For information about measurements see page 126.

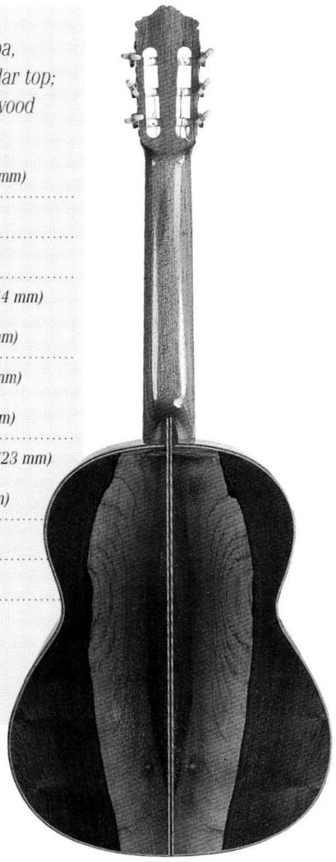

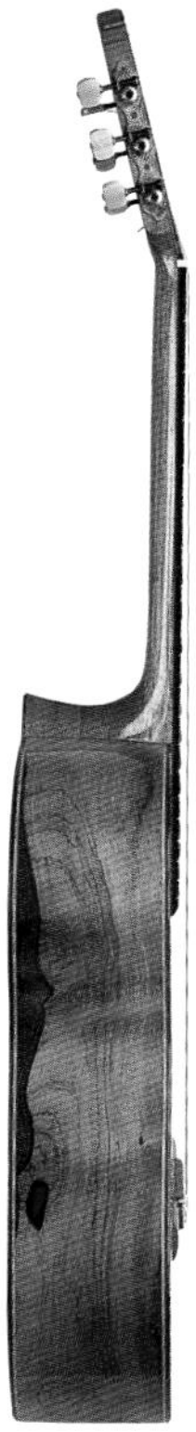

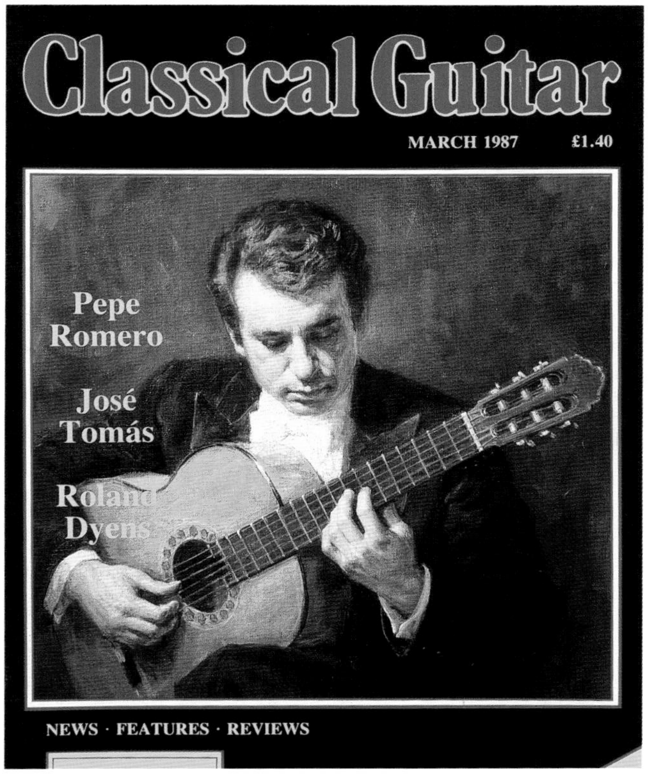

◄ Pepe Romero is seen on this magazine cover with a Rodríguez guitar, and also on the inset CD sleeve. (Pepe is on the far left, with Angel behind, Celin next to him, and the brothers' father Celedonio on the right.) The fine 1970s

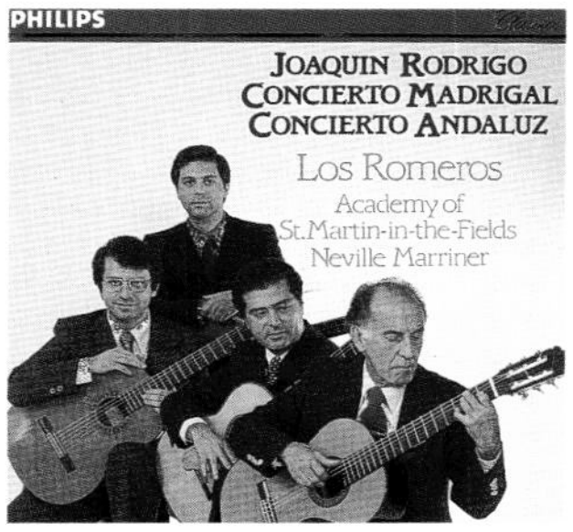

recording is of two pieces commissioned by the Romeros from Joaquín Rodrigo. Concierto Madrigal is based on a renaissance madrigal, while Rodrigo wrote of this performance of Concierto Andaluz: "The perfect conjunction of four guitarists sounding like one soloist."

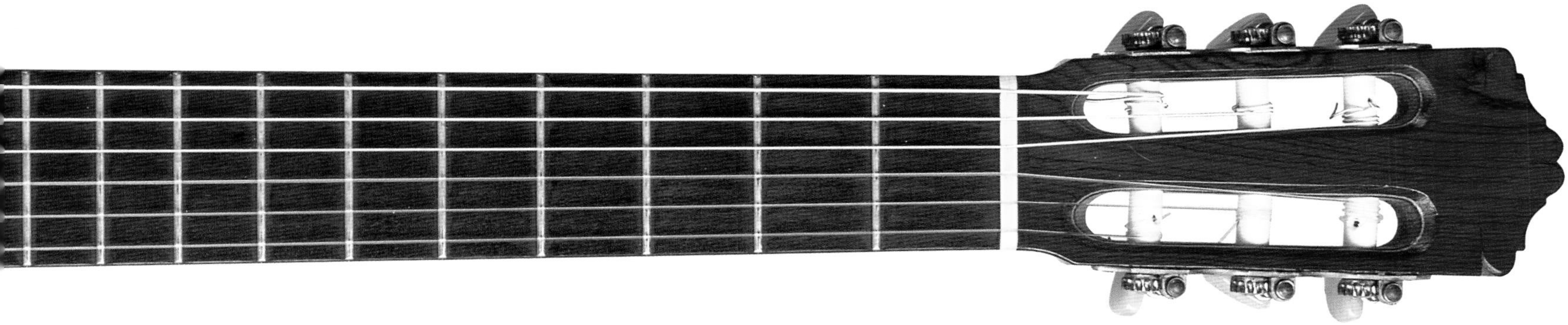

Miguel Rodríguez Beneyto was born in Cordóba in 1888. By the age of 15 he was playing string instruments, including guitars and bandurrias. Soon, under the influence of Rafael Casana (who in turn had been influenced by José Ramírez I) Rodríguez began making instruments, setting up shop in Calle Barberos around 1906. A few years later he moved to Calle San Fernando, and again in 1939 to a location on Alfaros where the Rodríguez workshop remains today.

His twin sons Miguel Jr. and Rafael were born in 1921, joining their father in the shop in 1933. Soon after this, the guitars became largely collaborative efforts. Miguel Sr. died in the mid 1970s. Rafael died tragically young in 1965, but Miguel Jr. continues to work on a very limited basis at the time of writing.

According to US guitar dealer Tim Miklaucic, "Rafael and Miguel Jr. both built guitars, but Rafael was a genius. He made many great guitars. I consider the Rodríguez family as a dynasty very close in importance to that of the Hauser family. They contributed guitars with a big sound, a cross between the southern Spanish and the European guitar, for large concert situations. Their guitars are very fast and have a flamenco feel, which players recognise as desirable, and have a beautiful tone. They're very Spanish, very musical."

The guitar here is one of a series known as the "church door" instruments, this example once being owned by Celedonio Romero. "They were made by my father," says Miguel Jr., although evidence suggests that other members of the family were also involved. "He was very interested in wood, and heard of a century-old door which was to be replaced by a new one, and bought it. The door was made of rosewood, probably from Brazil. He made one guitar at first which turned out well, and did several others."

"The 'church door' guitars are famous for their beauty, and for being from a very good period of Rodríguez," says Miklaucic. "They were allegedly made from the door of a church... but he probably just had a piece of wood that had a certain physical appearance that was very dramatic and very beautiful. The difference between a 'church door' and another Rodríguez is simply that the back and sides are made from certain slabs of Brazilian rosewood which contained a good deal of sapwood, which is the light-coloured wood that gives these dramatic contrasting features."

Miguel Rodríguez Jr. is proud of his family heritage. "Every maker has his own little secret twist, only truly appreciated by the public and the aficionados," he maintains. "Style develops with experience over many years. Most important is to have a good master, as I had," he says, referring to Miguel Sr. ● TONY BACON

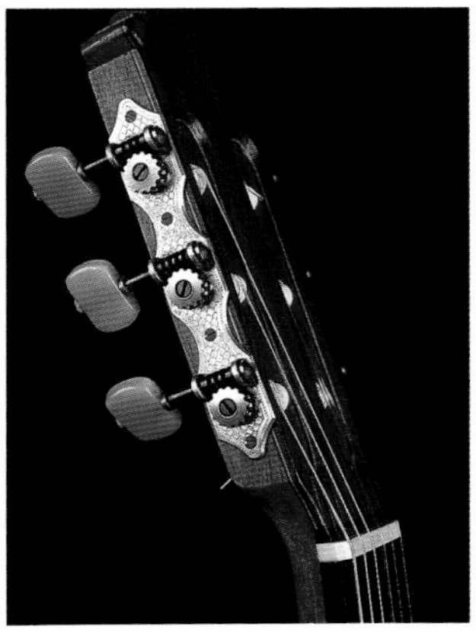

▲ The headstock of this Rodríguez instrument is fitted with a set of silver Landsdorder machine heads.

1978

Robert Ruck was born in 1945 in Milwaukee, Wisconsin, but grew up in Miami, Florida. At the age of 16 he chose to play classical and flamenco guitar. In high school he studied as a machinist which he credits as the source of his skills in accurate workmanship. In college he majored in art, but by this time the classical guitar was exerting much more influence over him and he soon abandoned college to enrol in the Milwaukee Conservatory of Music.

Ruck considers himself "musically challenged", and this self-assessment while studying for a career as a classical guitarist was probably one of the reasons he soon developed a desire to build instruments as well as play them. A friend taught him the fundamentals of fine woodworking, and Ruck began to make guitars without the benefit of an experienced guitar maker as mentor.

At the age of 20, guitar making was already Ruck's full-time occupation. At first his guitars were sold for low prices, as he later explained: "I sold them cheap for a long time to get them out there and to get feedback." Only after he had made about 100 guitars did the prices begin to reflect something closer to his instruments' true market value. He moved back to Wisconsin where he remained until 1990. Unlike most classical guitar builders, Ruck has made a wide range of wooden instruments more or less related to the guitar,

SPECIFICATIONS

Made by Ruck in the United States, 1978; serial number 162; spruce top; Brazilian rosewood back and sides (latter lined with spruce).

OVERALL LENGTH: 39⅛ ins (994 mm)

APPROX WEIGHT: 3⅝ lbs (1.6 kg)

SCALE LENGTH: 26¼ ins (667 mm)

STRING SPACING AT NUT: 1¾ ins (44 mm)

SPACING AT SADDLE: 2¼ ins (57 mm)

NECK WIDTH AT NUT: 2⅛ ins (54 mm)

WIDTH AT 12th FRET: 2½ ins (63 mm)

NECK DEPTH AT 1st FRET: ¹⁵⁄₁₆ ins (24 mm)

DEPTH AT 8th FRET: ¹⁵⁄₁₆ ins (24 mm)

BODY WIDTH: 14⁹⁄₁₆ ins (370 mm)

SIDE DEPTH: 3⅞ ins (98 mm)

✻ *For information about measurements see page 126.*

▶ *The Cuban guitarist Manuel Barrueco (sleeve, right), who has lived in the US since 1967, was a great and influential champion of Robert Ruck's guitars from the late 1960s. He began by using what Ruck described as "not in any way a special guitar" that he happened to pick up in Ruck's workshop. The Japanese guitarist Shin-ichi Fukuda recorded some of this 1991 album (far right) with a 1985 Ruck guitar.*

▼ **1978 RUCK**
Here is a fine example of a concert classical guitar built by Robert Ruck that is in excellent condition. Note especially the bold elegance of Ruck's red, black and blue rosette. The only signs of wear and tear are some small hairline cracks along the top on each side of the fingerboard. The top and bridge may have been French polished later, possibly by Ruck himself.

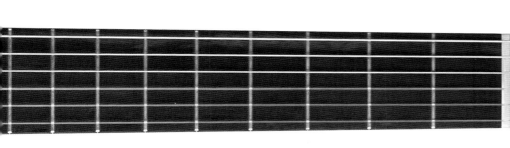

▼ *The simple label inside the soundhole of this fine instrument is signed, dated and serial-numbered by maker Robert Ruck, and also bears this American luthier's distinctive and unusual logo. In* addition – and beyond the ingenuity even *of our distinguished photographer – a deftly navigated mirror reveals that this particular guitar has been signed, dated and numbered underneath the top.*

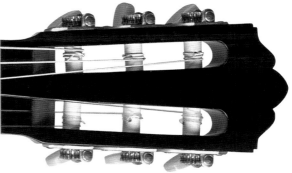

◀ *Robert Ruck once described his work thus: "I enter even the most mundane part of my work wholeheartedly, noticing the importance of every sawcut."*

including violas de gamba, vihuelas, and Renaissance, Baroque and Spanish lutes. His range of guitars is also impressive, including variations of the "extended" classical guitar with from seven to ten strings. During a career that stretches back over 30 years and more, Ruck reckons that he has constructed about 650 instruments, and all the while has managed to find the time to study classical and flamenco guitar playing.

Ruck has several standard models designed to meet the needs of a majority of classical players, but feels that his strong suit is an ability to build guitars custom-made for the individual, taking into consideration their personal requests and needs. After consulting with the player, he adjusts his patterns, bracing designs, woods and finishes, drawing from past experience to tailor a guitar that suits the customer.

In a 1992 lecture at the convention of the Guild of American Luthiers, Ruck explained his unusual approach to making custom guitars as a process that is both intuitive and practical. His shop is well outfitted with machine tools; these ensure accuracy and speed the initial preparation of the woods. Once past that point, Ruck clearly relishes the hands-on relationship between wood and woodworker, and relies on intuition informed by careful measurement

to achieve the sound he seeks for a particular instrument. Visualisation, a sort of active meditation on the desired result, is a part of his method. Ruck imagines at every step the sound he seeks from a guitar in progress – from choosing the wood, to working it, to completion in its new, musical form.

Ruck has many variables to choose from, and not only changes the top graduation and the size and pattern of the fan bracing, but alters the type of wood chosen for the braces as well. The same is true of finishes, and he uses French polish, varnish and a catalysed acrylic urethane, depending on the desired sound, on the guitar's woods, and the instrument's expected use.

Despite his somewhat unorthodox theories about the mental processes involved in building a classical guitar, Robert Ruck produces instruments that are quite traditional in appearance, something he attributes to being "brought up on the Spanish pattern". At the time of writing he lives and works north-west of Seattle in Washington, and his current output is about 30 finished guitars each year. ● **RICHARD JOHNSTON**

▲ *The headstock of this Ruck guitar is fitted with a set of machine heads made by Gotoh and finished in gold plate.*

1981

▶ The distinctive raised "elongated spear-head" motif on the headstock of Uruguayan guitarist Alvaro Pierri's instrument on the sleeve of this 1991 CD identifies it as the work of French guitar maker Daniel Friederich. Other recordings on Friederich guitars include Eduardo Fernández's Fernando Sor, Guitar Music album, also from 1991.

ALVARO
PIERRI
GITARRE
BROUWER • TORROBA
DE FALLA • HETU
GISMONTI

UNCONVENTIONAL GUITARS

Contreras was not the only maker to break with the traditions of the classical guitar and produce unusual, experimental instruments. A small number of makers toyed with the size of the guitar in the mid to late 19th century, offering a range of guitars designated the terz (tuned a minor third higher than the normal instrument), the quarte (tuned a fourth higher) and the quinte-basse (a fifth below). Apparently the terz was relatively popular; Guiliani went so far as to compose a concerto for terz guitar. In Britain around the 1870s Madame Sidney Pratten, an enterprising guitarist and teacher, designed a terz guitar that she named the Bambina or "baby" guitar, with a string-length just a little over half the normal. The Bambina was intended as an easy-to-play first instrument for Pratten's many pupils in and around London.

Another idea that has tempted some players and builders from the familar path is that of the "extended" guitar, an instrument with more than the now-standard complement of six strings. The principle of six single strings had been gradually established around 1800 in Europe, evolving from the previously typical five courses, or double strings, of many earlier guitars. By the time Torres began his crucial work in the 1850s, six strings were well accepted as the norm for the guitar. Yet around the 1870s Torres made at least three 11-string guitars. These appear to have had five extra bass

strings. The beautiful sound of one such Torres, heard in a recital given by Giménez Manjón in 1889, is said to have persuaded Miguel Llobet to a musical career.

An extreme example of the multi-stringed instrument came from a contemporary of Torres, though hardly as important a maker: one José Gallegos of Malaga, who showed his "guitarpa" at London's Great Exhibition of 1851. The one-off instrument had 35 strings, but from the exhibition catalogue's description it seems merely to have been an odd combination of guitar, harp and cello, retaining six strings for the guitar section. Such combinations of instruments enjoyed a vogue in the 19th century. Before and especially just after 1800 the lyre guitar and the harp guitar followed the contemporary neo-classical trend, combining a guitar with the ancient Greek lyre and with the classical harp.

Probably the best known player of a multi-string classical guitar was the Spanish guitarist Narciso Yepes (1927-1997) who constantly deployed a ten-string instrument from the mid

1960s. Yepes told Larry Snitzler in 1978 that he had wanted a ten-string guitar because he found the six-string instrument "unbalanced". He felt that only certain fretted notes on the six-string produced sympathetic vibrations in the other strings, whereas a ten-string guitar would spread this pleasant effect to further notes. "I can stop the resonance," Yepes said, "but only because I have it in the first place. Also, if I have a ten-string guitar, it includes a six-string guitar," he said, "but if I have a six-string guitar, I do not have a ten-string. So I think I have all the advantages and none of the inconveniences." Despite this stirring manifesto, few others used the ten-string instrument, and the six-string classical guitar continues to reign. ● TONY BACON

● English guitar player Paul Gregory shows off his de la Cruz guitar (left) which has extra soundholes either side of the waist, plus a soundhole 'rose' that is often encountered on early guitars. In the centre sleeve is shown a ten-string guitar of Narciso Yepes, who played mainly Ramirez and Bernabé guitars. Scottish guitarist Simon Wynberg (right) is one of only a handful of other players to use a ten-string.

firmly on old, accepted ideas of construction. "When I was a kid I used to love the films of Charlie Chaplin," he told Clinton. "I admired the antique cars... but I think it is normal for me to drive a good modern car, travel by plane, have TV and so on, all the things we have in our modern life. And in my work too it is natural that the modern world is reflected. I respect the work of Torres as much as anyone else, and if I had been living in his time, I would have imitated him. I would even have tried to improve what he did, because that is the way I am. Torres achieved everything because he was anything but conservative. If he were living today I think he would have understood my discontents."

Contreras's industry did attract a number of awards over the years, and these have included the Madrid Chamber of Commerce's *Merito Artesano* Export Award and, underlining his popularity in France, City Medals from Salon-de-Provence and Digne as well as an Order Of The Gold Rosette from the Isla de la Francia Guitar Circle.

The Carlevaro model, as shown on these pages, was first made by Contreras in 1983, based on an idea brought to him by a Uruguayan guitarist, Abel Carlevaro. The two got together in 1980 and began to discuss a guitar design that incorporated a number of unusual elements, again with the intention of increasing the

instrument's sound projection. The inspiration for the missing waist on the bass side of the Carlevaro and its lack of a soundhole was the assumption that more air volume inside the guitar's body and a larger vibrating area on top would increase its volume. Rather than the double top of Contreras's earlier effort, the Carlevaro design has an extra set of sides and back "around" the body to isolate it from the damping effect of the player's body.

This latter idea was taken further in an experimental guitar that Contreras made in the mid 1980s for American guitarist Antonio Mendoza. A visitor to the workshop at the time – who noted the presence of three full-time workers in addition to Contreras – described the resulting instrument as "a sort of casing holding the guitar inside in suspension". The Romeros became firm supporters of the Mendoza design in the late 1980s.

"I am not looking to improve the shape of the guitar, because I love its traditional lines," Contreras insisted. "But it must be said that beauty is one thing, the sound another. I must tell you that what I am trying to do is to achieve in the present what will be the guitar of the future. And if I can't achieve that then I'll try to find a way that might be a guide to others yet to come." After Manuel Contreras's recent death, his son Paulo continues the business. ● TONY BACON

▲ The machine heads are a fine set of gold-plated and engraved Fusteros, as originally fitted, with a typical lyre motif at the top of the backing plate.

Hermann Hauser III took over the family business upon the death of his father, Hauser II, in 1988. He had started building guitars much earlier, making his first in 1974. At the age of 15, Hauser III had started an apprenticeship with a local stringed-instrument maker, and after he had won the highest national awards for apprentices he attended a school for instrument building in Mittenwald, the traditional German centre of violin and guitar making.

At the same time, in 1978, Hauser III began to work in his father's company. "I had to start all over again with instrument building," he says. "The most important influence on my work and my career was my father's teaching." He learned to build guitars by hand, for a certain sound. It wasn't easy for Hauser III to follow in the footsteps of such an illustrious father and grandfather. "In the beginning," Hauser recalls, "when I started building guitars, a lot of people kept saying, 'Well, the boy... he doesn't know anything. His guitars are not that good.' I got the feeling that I had to be two or three times as good to become as respected as other builders who had started their own businesses."

American guitar dealer Tim Miklaucic, who knows the Hauser family, says that in the US too there was initial wariness about Hauser III guitars. "There was a sense that he was just the grandson

of someone great, but not great himself," says Miklaucic. "But if he hadn't been Hauser III, a dealer like me would have considered his guitars a real find. And despite all that, I think that Hauser III has made guitars equal to those of his father and his grandfather."

The responsibility of the family tradition meant that it was more difficult for Hauser III to develop his own style. It took him some years to find the right balance between the traditional Hauser features and his own ideas, which emerge now in fine details rather than the overall look of the guitars. Hauser's constructional methods have tended to follow the traditions of his grandfather and father, from whom he has also inherited a considerable quantity of excellent wood, including a collection of fine spruce over 80 years old and Brazilian rosewood up to 60 years old.

Hauser III has made more than 400 guitars, and at the time of writing makes between 12 and 18 a year. Two other people come to the workshop for a number of hours a week to do minor work like sanding, and there is also Hans Hasenfranz ("Hasi"). "He was an assistant to his father [Hauser II] as well," says Miklaucic. "One reason that there is so much continuity in the guitars of the Hausers is because Hasi has been there through the generations." Hauser III says that a good guitar is a compromise between loudness, balance

► Hermann Hauser III was born in 1958, made his first guitar in 1974, and took over the family business upon the death of his father, Hauser II, in 1988.

▼ 1988 HAUSER III
This well-made guitar is evidence of some of the changes made to the traditional Hauser instrument by the grandson of the originator. For example, Hauser III has used a top of western red cedar, underneath which is a stronger central fan brace. Also inside the instrument is a neck extension that is designed to improve the upper-treble response of the guitar. At the time of writing Hauser III offers three main types of guitar: a "Segovia" model, based on the instrument his grandfather made for Segovia in the 1930s; a "Bream" model, based on a Hauser I guitar that Bream asked Hauser III to copy; and his own "Dream" model, which combines some of the features of the previous two. Demand is generally greatest for the "Segovia".

◄ The label of this mint-condition guitar is signed by Hermann Hauser III, and is also numbered and dated. Unlike the earlier Hauser labels that we have already encountered earlier in the book (see page 37 and page 60), this example of the modern Hauser III label has the workshop location printed as Reisbach, and goes on to mention the fact that the business was previously located in Munich ("früher München"). This particular instrument is also signed, dated and numbered on the interior neck extension. Hauser III works on his guitars within the cycle of a year; rather, he says, "like a farmer". Thus he selects the wood in October, makes the guitar bodies in winter when the air is dry, and finishes the instruments in the summer. One guitar that Hauser III built recently is especially close to his heart. "It is not a normal guitar... it's a monster!" he exclaims. "It has everything that I would like to create in a guitar. It is quite loud, plus it is very balanced, and very clear. I could never part with it."

SPECIFICATIONS
Made by Hauser III in Reisbach, Germany, 1988; serial number 207; western red cedar top; Brazilian rosewood back and sides.

OVERALL LENGTH: 38⅜ ins (975 mm)

APPROX WEIGHT: 3½ lbs (1.6 kg)

SCALE LENGTH: 25½ ins (648 mm)

STRING SPACING AT NUT: 1²³⁄₃₂ ins (44 mm)

SPACING AT SADDLE: 2⁹⁄₃₂ ins (58 mm)

NECK WIDTH AT NUT: 2¹⁄₁₆ ins (52 mm)

WIDTH AT 12th FRET: 2½ ins (63 mm)

NECK DEPTH AT 1st FRET: ²⁷⁄₃₂ ins (21 mm)

DEPTH AT 8th FRET: ¹³⁄₁₆ ins (24 mm)

BODY WIDTH: 14⁹⁄₁₆ ins (370 mm)

SIDE DEPTH: 4¹⁄₁₆ ins (103 mm)

✧ For information about measurements see page 126.

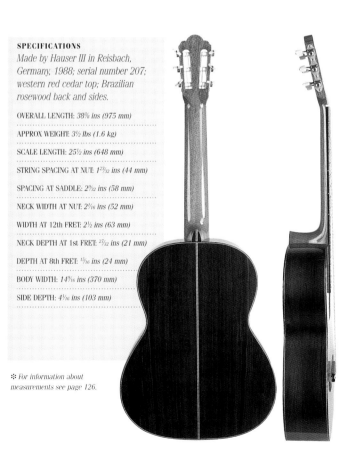

and tone quality. He chooses wood for its inherent resonant frequency. "Today, most of my guitars are made from tonewoods with a resonant frequency of g or g#, which seems the best compromise," reports Hauser.

Hauser III did build one guitar for Segovia, shortly before the great guitarist's death in 1987, and has made several test models for Julian Bream. Guitarists who have played Hauser III guitars include Pepe and Angel Romero, Akinobu Matsuda in Japan, Argentinean guitarist Manuel López Ramos, and the Folkwang Duo.

Hauser III deplores the demand today for guitars that are simply loud. As he puts it: "The louder the guitar, the bigger the lack of character." Loud guitars have less dynamic headroom, to Hauser's ears. They sound piano-like but lack that instrument's potential for damping. They create too many overtones, have less clarity and balance, and, Hauser suggests, may not last very long. "A guitarist gives every single note as a gift to his audience. The tone reaches to their hearts, not just the ears. So you don't have to be loud when you give these gifts to your audience – they will hear." It's unsurprising, then, that Hauser's guitars are not the loudest on the market. But their ability to project, Hermann Hauser maintains, is a quality "that makes a great guitar even greater". ● **HEINZ REBELLIUS/GRAHAM WADE**

▲ The headstock of this Hauser III instrument is fitted with a set of silver Landsdorfer machine heads, with mother-of-pearl buttons.

(1960-73) and deputised for Segovia at the Santiago de Compostela Summer Courses in 1961 and 1962. Each year he made more recordings, destined in time to cover the range of the existing guitar repertoire (and ultimately extended its possibilities with new works written for him by composers such as Torroba, Dodgson, Previn and Takemitsu). His concerts, whether solo or with orchestra, were universally

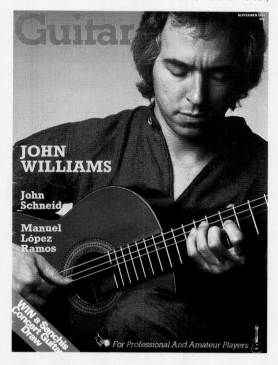

● On the Virtuoso Music For Guitar sleeve (right) John Williams is seen with his 1961 Fleta guitar, while on the 1983 Guitar magazine (above), the Echoes Of Spain sleeve (left) and the Barrios cover (far right) he is playing a 1972 instrument from the same maker. Since the early 1980s Williams has forsaken his Fleta guitars for instruments made by Greg Smallman, as used on the Takemitsu record (right, centre).

greeted with admiration bordering on incredulity by guitarists, public and critics alike. Thus began his illustrious international career, his tours now reaching out to Australia, the Far East, North and South America, and throughout Europe. But around 1973 the appeal of the road diminished and Williams cut down the number of his recitals considerably.

This break with the artist's customary nomadic existence was an essential aspect of Williams' apparently unconventional development at that time. It coincided with a move to dispense with the traditional concert attire of a player (a sartorial shift from the dinner jacket to the guru shirt), and the emergence of musical opinions quite different from a good number of his fellow leading classical artists.

Many of Williams' more unconventional activities have succeeded in bringing the guitar to the widest possible audience. He believes that the wrong questions are often asked about the role of classical music and the guitar itself. In an interview with him for Guitar Review in 1994, Jim Tosone enquired about the problem of a diminishing public, citing a New York radio station "unable to retain serious listeners of classical music or attract a large enough general audience". Williams, perhaps unexpectedly, focused on the multiplicity of music in modern society rather than the image of classical music at bay against a hostile world: "I think as soon as you select classical guitar music and assume that there is something intrinsically good about there being more of it for a hypothetical audience that you want to improve, you're putting up a whole lot of assumptions about what should be done, which I'm afraid I can't do. I can't say it's better that Britten or Takemitsu wrote this wonderful piece for guitar and we as serious guitarists are playing it, and we want more people to listen to it. I can't honestly say that is more significant than the jazz group around the corner at the

club or The Chieftains at a folk music festival. We as classical players should try and learn from and be part of it." Few contemporary classical musicians have succeeded in an era when popular music is commercially powerful and unprecedentedly influential in people's lives, to cross over to the widest possible audience and at the same time retain their artistic integrity. But John Williams has been predominant for years in this area, setting the highest standards.

Williams has of course, despite his own comments, spent his career demonstrating what many people find "intrinsically good" within the European musical tradition. His flawless performances of the music of J.S. Bach, Domenico Scarlatti, Agustín Barrios Mangoré (whose music he rescued from neglect), Isaac Albéniz, Petrassi, Takemitsu, Rodrigo's Concierto de Aranjuez, and a multitude of other works from the 16th century to the present day, have created criteria against which all guitarists will be assessed. His personal contribution to the guitar is overwhelming and awe-inspiring, a unique monument to phenomenal virtuosity and musicianship. Over 50 recorded albums, as well as hundreds of recitals and broadcasts, bear witness to an extraordinarily

consistent quality of output maintained over 40 years of a dazzling and perpetually ascending career. His achievement has been to emphasise that a perfect mastery of that difficult instrument, the guitar, is possible and essential. In this he has been a unique source of inspiration and wonder for both players and public. ● GRAHAM WADE

necessary support to the front, yet without impeding its flexibility."

Smallman told the guitarist that he found the traditional fan-strut bracing inclined to impede the vibration of a guitar top, restricting the crucial movement of the central zone, while his lattice strutting increases the vibrating area. The guitar maker then showed Byzantine his method for "tuning" guitar tops, which he begins by inserting the top to be adjusted into a dummy instrument. "Once this is in place and strung up, he taps the front in seven precise places and correspondingly then plucks a note with which each tap should coincide. If it does not, he then adds more or less weight to the strut at that particular point until corrected. I am not sure how he conceived this idea, but he maintains it is the best way to balance a front, and will ensure greater evenness and reduction in 'short' (dead) notes." Byzantine was surprised to see Smallman during the "tuning" process using small pieces of Blu-Tack, a clay-like re-usable adhesive originated by Bostik, to add weight where a resonance problem occurs.

Byzantine was clearly impressed by what he saw and heard, and remains at the time of writing a confirmed Smallman player. In his report he praised the guitars' ease of playability and their outstanding projectional qualities, describing the overall sound as

rich and dark yet clear and even. "Perhaps his guitar may not have the intimacy of sound which might appeal to some players," he wrote. "This is not so much a criticism but more to do with the nature of his instruments, as Smallman definitely has the concert hall and not the drawing room in mind."

Smallman makes a small number of guitars each year at very high prices, and the waiting list for his instruments is very long indeed. The list of players extends from the Hill-Wiltschinsky Duo to Paul McCartney. Smallman's success has inspired quite a few other Australian makers to apply his design ideas and build classical guitars, and a number of the apprentices who have passed through Smallman's workshop now make instruments in their own right, including Eugene Philp (who was initially responsible for the remarkable Smallman hardwood cases) and Ian Kneipp.

A final word from John Williams, without whom it is unlikely that too many players would ever have heard of Greg Smallman. "What I find interesting and wonderful about Greg's approach," said Williams in 1993, "is that he starts from admiring the traditional – not knocking it, but wanting to know if it's possible to improve it in some way. He has quite clearly done that for me. Basically, he is making the guitar a more musical instrument." ● TONY BACON

SCIENCE AND THE GUITAR MAKER

For all its vigour, a vibrating guitar string itself is a very poor radiator of sound. It is simply too small to interact with the air to create the local pressure changes which are the origin of sound waves. The acoustical function of the guitar body is to act as a mechanical amplifier, enhancing the transfer of vibrational energy from the string into sound. As the vibrating string swings to and fro it pulls and pushes on the bridge, and this oscillating force sets up sympathetic vibrations of the entire guitar body. Although the motion of the soundboard and body shell is far too small to be seen, their large surface area ensures efficient coupling to the surrounding air. It is these vibrations of the wooden structure, driven by the string, which generate the sound waves we hear.

The motion of a plucked string is far more complex than it appears at first sight. Plucking the string simultaneously

excites its various modes of vibration. It is important to understand more about these modes of vibration because we will use a similar concept when describing the motion of the guitar body. We can get a feel for string modes by playing with a "slinky spring" stretched between two hands (Figure 1). Try this experiment yourself. The spring vibrates in an identical way to a stretched string, but the lower tension and increased mass of the spring slows down the motion. Instead of letting the string (or spring) vibrate freely, we can force it to vibrate by gently wobbling our hand up and down. When the string is vibrated at just the right rate, at one of its resonant frequencies, we can excite individual modes, producing lots of movement for little effort.

In its fundamental mode (Figure 1a), the string simply oscillates up and down. It is the repetition rate of this mode which effectively governs the pitch of the sound, which, as we know from experience, depends on the tension and the vibrating length and mass of the string. If oscillated at two, three or four times the fundamental frequency, the string hops into one of its higher modes of vibration, each of which involves progressively more complex motion. Although the envelope of the motion of a plucked string looks superficially like the fundamental mode, plucking excites all the modes together, simultaneously driving the guitar body at several

frequencies. This mix of sounds constitutes a guitar note.

In an ideal string, the modes vibrate at integer multiples of the fundamental and generate harmonic frequencies. (The term "harmonic" is used in a more specialised way by scientists than musicians. Here we can take it to mean the individual frequency components created by the string.) This is a highly desirable feature, because under these circumstances the ear blends the individual sounds to give the perception of just one note, with a clearly-defined pitch and a timbre which is related to the relative intensities and the decay rates of the harmonics. In fact, string stiffness (particularly problematic on the third string) and coupling effects with the body tend to make the modes slightly anharmonic (not harmonic), affecting sound "clarity". Players have considerable scope to modify timbre by altering the mix of harmonics by plucking the string at different places along

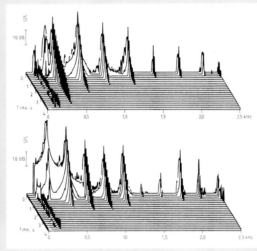

● **Figure 1** (left: a top, b middle, c below). First three modes of vibration of a stretched string. **Figure 2** (centre) Sound spectra of open guitar string notes: (a top) 1st string; (b below) 2nd string. Vertical axis shows sound intensity; horizontal axis frequency; axis toward the reader increasing time. The decaying peaks are string harmonics. **Figure 3** (right) A mode of vibration visualised using holographic interferometry. The "contour lines" map out the vibration of the soundboard.

its length or altering amounts of nail/flesh used in the attack. The string harmonics can be seen as tall, equally-spaced peaks in Figure 2; the harmonics decay partly through friction losses and partly through useful radiation of sound.

The same basic principles which govern the vibrations of strings also apply to the body of the guitar. Unfortunately, it is not so easy to detect the vibrational modes of the body because the motion is so small. Holographic techniques can be used to create "contour maps" of modes (as shown in Figure 3), but for our present purposes we would be better to concentrate on Figure 5, which shows some computer simulations of the modal vibrations of a guitar soundboard.

The lowest mode induces large volume changes in the air and is thus an excellent radiator of sound. We also see, from the motion of the bridge, that the strings readily couple to this mode. By coupling, we mean that the string and body find it easy to exchange energy. The same is true, though to a lesser extent, of the third and fourth modes (Figures 5c and 5d). One point which is generally not appreciated is that these strongly-coupled "air-pumping" modes are responsible for radiating much of the guitar's energy at all frequencies. However, to be good radiators at high frequencies, it is essential that the vibrating mass of the soundboard be kept as low as possible, requiring a thin, well-supported plate.

Many of the higher modes are less effective radiators or are unable to couple to the strings and play a much less important role in determining the quality of the instrument. What we must understand, however, is that the precise shape of these modes, their radiation efficiencies and the ease with which they couple to the strings are *unique* to each instrument and are determined by the materials, design and construction of the instrument. The exact form of the body modes is what ultimately controls a guitar's tone quality.

The soundboard is undoubtedly the single most important part of the instrument. Makers choose materials for soundboards very carefully, ensuring that they have inherently high stiffness and low density, two factors which combine to enhance the amount of sound radiated from the instrument. The stiffness-to-mass ratio of the soundboard is further optimised by using a thin plate stiffened by the internal struts

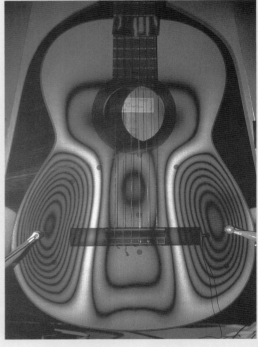

and by the bridge. This optimisation is particularly important today because of the requirement to build guitars powerful enough for performances in large concert halls. Materials for other parts are far less critical. The back and sides are normally made from dense hardwoods, chosen as much for visual impact as acoustical criteria. The back is not a "reflector" of sound, but vibrates and radiates sound in a similar way to the soundboard. However, heavy materials limit the vibrations of the back and help to reduce the inevitable loss of vibrational energy which occurs through contact with the player. The body cavity also plays its part, most importantly to enhance sound radiation at low frequencies.

The makers' reappraisal of the role of the soundboard and its strutting – both the internal fan strutting and the external bridge – were the key to the development of the modern guitar. There are two complementary requirements of strutting systems. The strutted plate must have sufficient static strength to prevent distortion and premature failure under the action of the sizeable torque exerted by modern, high-tension strings. On the other hand, the soundboard must retain sufficient dynamic flexibility to respond to the vibrations of the strings. The balance between plate size, thickness and stiffness must be carefully regulated if the acoustical advantages are to be maximised.

It is often supposed that a larger plate will make more sound, but an increase in size requires an increase in thickness of the plate to retain its strength, and the consequential increase in mass might lead to a reduction in sound output, particularly at higher frequencies. (This is why large instruments often become bass heavy or "boomy".) The relative merits of various strutting systems or individual approaches to guitar construction continue to be a hotly-debated subject among makers.

Returning to Figure 5 enables us to appreciate the specific role played by different components of the soundboard. The soundboard clearly vibrates as a whole with the majority of the activity occurring in the lower bout. The bridge is an extremely important element of the guitar, and design variations can be used to induce substantial changes in the vibrating properties of the instrument and to fine-tune

strategic point which tends to lower the frequencies of modes (particularly the fourth mode). In this same guitar, a small bar was added running under the treble side of the bridge (like Rubio's "nodal" bar) adding asymmetry into the vibrations. Asymmetry can help enhance sound radiation from modes such as Figure 5b, but the effect is relatively small. (Modes which involve equal inward and outward displacement are naturally poor radiators of sound because they induce no volume change in the air as they vibrate.) Another method for adding asymmetry is to employ an angled harmonic bar below the soundhole (as done by Ramírez). What is much more important, however, is the subtle change in the position of the nodal line, which has moved to the left towards the sixth string. As the node moves, it alters the efficiency of the string-body coupling. Controlling the modes' shapes, and hence the coupling

as being louder or that it has greater "presence". When the coupling becomes too strong, the string ceases to be the dominant partner, with disastrous consequences.

The fundamental string component in Figure 2b shows the effects of "over-coupling" – it "dies" very rapidly. Worse still, the string mode is shifted out of tune with respect to the higher harmonics and produces a most unpleasant sound. The lowest few modes of the guitar are highly susceptible to this problem, and any responsive guitar will produce a few "wolf-notes", usually to be found on the lower reaches of the fourth string. Modern trends in guitar making appear to exacerbate this problem, which, in the opinion of the author, produces guitars which sound loud but lack the purity and sustain of more controlled instruments. Here is a dilemma: a compliant soundboard is essential for good response across the playing range of the instrument, but we necessarily trade

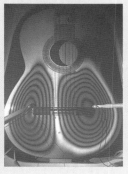
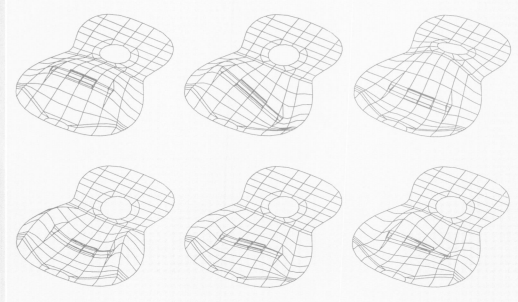

● **Figure 4** *(far left: a top, b below) shows the effects of modifications of the internal strutting (see text).*
Figure 5 *(left: a,b,c; d,e,f below) shows computer simulations of six modes of a Torres-style soundboard. They take into account the material properties of the plate and struts, the strutting layout, and shape of the bridge, accurately modelling modes seen in real life. The resonance frequencies of the modes depend on the size of the plate, its stiffness and its vibrating mass, but those shown here typically fall in the range of 150 to 800 Hz. As with the string, the motion of the plate gets progressively more complex at higher frequencies, splitting into smaller and smaller vibrating regions separated by non-moving lines, or nodes, but the resonance frequencies are no longer so simply related.*

the instrument's response. We see that in the lower modes (Figures 5a-c) the bridge acts almost as if it were a rigid bar; above about 500 Hz (Figure 5d) it starts to bend and twist. The internal structure is also important. The fan braces and harmonic bars add stiffness without adding much additional mass. The fan struts do not substantially influence the shapes of the modes until very high frequencies. Their function is to achieve the correct balance between longitudinal and transverse stiffness of the plate, but their precise number and distribution are of less importance. The acoustical role of the harmonic bars, like that of the bridge, is often underestimated. Because they lie across the grain, in a direction where the spruce plate might be ten times or more less stiff than along the grain, modifications to their dimensions can have very radical effects on the mechanical action of the instrument.

Detailed design changes alter the resonance frequencies and the precise shapes of the modes to give each instrument its unique character. By way of an example, Figure 4 shows the first two modes of a guitar in which the harmonic bars have been relieved on either side of the soundhole (such as the Bouchet system). Contrary to popular belief, this does not significantly extend the vibrations into the upper bout. However, the cut-outs reduce the stiffness of the plate at this

between the strings and body, is the key to controlling the tone quality of the instrument.

Investigations of a large number of instruments show that all guitars of "standard" construction share the basic features discussed above. Indeed, even "novel" or non-standard construction techniques produce similar mechanical action; there have been no developments of the classical guitar which have fundamentally altered the way it works. What distinguishes one instrument from another or the great from the mediocre are the detailed differences, however small.

We have seen that the body of the guitar is the means by which the string (and the player) communicates with the outside world. Efficient transfer of energy from the strings depends firstly on good coupling to the body and secondly on good radiation efficiency of the body modes. The coupling between the strings and the body must be very carefully regulated, however, if the maker is to achieve a "good" sound. The standard text-book string begins to depart rapidly from its simple behaviour when it is mounted on a compliant support. As the coupling increases, the radiated harmonics of the string increase in initial intensity but decay more rapidly – our single shot of energy which we put into the string is used up faster. You would be wrong to imagine that this more intense but rapidly decaying sound is necessarily perceived

off good response with poor sustain and "false" notes. There are no simple solutions to this dilemma, nor is there a strutting pattern which guarantees success in resolving the subtle balancing act that is required in the production of a top-quality instrument. The production of the best guitars involves making compromises and choices – there is no unique formula for creating a "perfect" instrument. Makers tend to use an empirical approach, with varied success, to explore a problem which has seemingly infinite variables.

One of the most interesting recent developments is the use of lattice bracing (such as that employed by Smallman), an approach firmly bedded in good acoustical principles. By stiffening the wood across the grain with a lattice-work of delicate struts one is able to work the soundboard much thinner than usual while retaining stiffness, thereby increasing that all-important stiffness-to-mass ratio of the plate. The vibrating mass of the soundboard is kept low, increasing sound radiation, but mode frequencies are kept high, which helps tame the effects of over-strong coupling. This is all good acoustical theory, but the approach yields a character-istically different sound which is not liked by everyone. Only time will tell whether or not such methods will be used more routinely. Ultimately, it is that all-discerning individual, the player, who will decide. ● **BERNARD RICHARDSON**

▼ **1993 HUMPHREY MILLENNIUM**
This is a fine contemporary classical instrument made by one of the leading American builders of today, Thomas Humphrey, using his distinctive Millennium design. The most visually evident feature of the design is an angled top and "negative" neck angle. "By sloping the soundboard and using a high neck angle," Humphrey told Acoustic Guitar magazine, "an entirely different load is created on the soundboard, producing greater power. The elevated fingerboard, which results from the high neck angle, allows incredible access to the upper register."

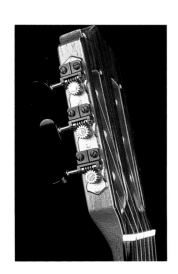

▲ The Gilbert guitar's headstock has an elegant pointed tip, and is fitted with a set of gold-plated, ebony-button machine heads made to Gilbert's own functional-looking design. This is quite unusual; most makers buy tuners of a proprietary brand from a specialist supplier.

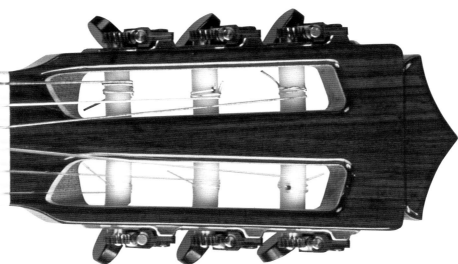

▲ John Gilbert (left) began building guitars as a hobby in the 1960s, moving to guitar making full-time in 1974. His son William (right) joined his father in 1991 and today builds guitars under his own name. John pursues other projects such as the design of machine heads.

string would have a long job on a conventional bridge, where the height of all six strings is determined by a single saddle. "With the pins, *voilà*! You say, 'I'd like to have this string a little higher.' Fine. Just take the string off the pin, lift the pin up by a wafer and put the string back. It takes less than one minute."

The years of experience in high-tech engineering gave Gilbert a definite attitude when it came to working with wood. Rather than submit to the material's reputation for inconsistency and instability, he instead chose to lessen the effects of those attributes by careful measurement, not only of the wood's dimensions but of its weight and stiffness as well. This was combined with meticulous record-keeping and careful experimentation, leaving nothing to chance. When trying something new he would strive to keep the rest of the guitar the same as previous examples, so that he could accurately assess the effects of the change.

He has also assessed the great makers' work, in typically methodical style. "I used to build my guitar very much like Fleta," he told Magnussen. "And I had a maker visit me who said, 'You'll never build a good guitar with nine struts.' And I thought to myself, you should have told that to Fleta... When I was repairing I'd do anything, as long as I could work on someone's guitar. And I'd look inside,

study them, make drawings of them, say, 'Why did this guy do that?' Finally you start to see things, and develop your own methods."

He took the string action on his guitars with equal seriousness, gaining a reputation for a close action and a clean tone. Rather than searching for sound with a certain character, Gilbert says he "builds a machine", and that he strives for a neutral response. With a reputation for consistency, both from one instrument to another and from the lowest to the highest fret, his instruments are intended as vehicles for the player's artistry. Guitarists such as David Russell, Fred Hand and David Tanenbaum found these "machines" of wood to be excellent – if unforgiving – tools of expression.

By 1991, as Gilbert approached the age of 70, he had built 140 guitars. His son William (Bill) then joined him and the two worked together for some time, with both signing the labels. Bill now builds under his own name, leaving his father to pursue other projects such as a line of machine heads for the classical guitar. John Gilbert has lectured widely about his methods of guitar making, stressing a number of unromantic notions such as careful measurement, controlled experiments and unrelenting precision. More than one young luthier has been startled by a revealing question from him, such as, "How much does your bridge weigh?" ● RICHARD JOHNSTON

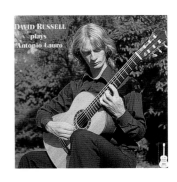

▲ Scottish-born guitarist David Russell grew up on the Spanish island of Minorca, moving to London in the late 1960s where he began a successful career as a talented young guitarist. This 1980 album of music by the Venezuelan guitarist and composer Antonio Lauro, on which Russell plays a Gilbert guitar, was recorded before Russell's later move to Spain, where he now lives.

1996

SPECIFICATIONS
*Made by Romanillos in Semley,
England, 1996; number 747;
European spruce top; Indian
rosewood back and sides.*

OVERALL LENGTH: *39 ins (991 mm)*

APPROX WEIGHT: *3¼ lbs (1.5 kg)*

SCALE LENGTH: *25¾ ins (654 mm)*

STRING SPACING AT NUT: *1²⁵⁄₃₂ ins (45 mm)*

SPACING AT SADDLE: *2¼ ins (57 mm)*

NECK WIDTH AT NUT: *2³⁄₃₂ ins (53 mm)*

WIDTH AT 12th FRET: *2¹⁷⁄₃₂ ins (64 mm)*

NECK DEPTH AT 1st FRET: *⅞ ins (22 mm)*

DEPTH AT 8th FRET: *1 ins (25 mm)*

BODY WIDTH: *14⁷⁄₁₆ ins (367mm)*

SIDE DEPTH: *3¹⁵⁄₁₆ ins (100 mm)*

✻ *For information about
measurements see page 126.*

José Luis Romanillos Vega was born in 1932 in Madrid. A cabinet maker by trade and an enthusiastic amateur guitarist, he moved to England in 1956 and built a guitar for his own use in 1959. Encouraged by the response of other guitarists to his first instrument, he developed his craft over the next few years.

After a three-year period in Spain, José Romanillos returned to England in 1967. A number of London-based guitarists, notably Carlos Bonell and Gilbert Biberian, expressed strong interest in Romanillos' most recent instruments, and it was at this point he gave up his regular job to pursue a full-time career in guitar making.

He showed one of his guitars to Julian Bream in 1970, and a long-standing performer/luthier relationship was immediately forged. With Bream's support, Romanillos was able to set up a workshop close to Bream's home in the Dorset village of Semley. Over the next two decades, Bream continued to take a close interest in the development of Romanillos guitars. A BBC documentary from the mid 1970s shows Romanillos at work on one of Bream's guitars, and the majority of Bream's RCA recordings from this period were made using Romanillos guitars. The British Channel 4 TV series *Guitarra* also featured Bream playing a vihuela and a five-course Baroque guitar, both of which were built for him

▼ 1996 ROMANILLOS
A beautifully elegant and well-crafted concert classical guitar made by José and Liam Romanillos. This is one of Romanillos' smaller, Torres-inspired instruments. The lower harmonic bar of its internal strutting has been cut out to allow the two outer "fan" struts to pass

under it, thus extending the available soundboard area. Subtle touches like the rosette (in Romanillos' familiar "Moorish arch" style, inspired by the mosque at Córdoba), and the exquisite headstock inlay, underline an instrument of grace and charm which is in superb, virtually unplayed condition.

◄ *This astonishing record transports to the listener the sound of Julian Bream, his Romanillos guitar and the wondrous acoustic of Wardour Chapel in Wiltshire. The transcriptions of the piano music of Granados and Albéniz are familiar now through many other performances, but few as magical and affecting as this.*

▶ *José Romanillos, a native of Madrid, first moved to England in the 1950s, and began building guitars full-time in the 1960s. Recently his son Liam (pictured behind him, right) joined José in the business. The two are shown in the workshop together in the photograph below. The label (left) of this 1996 instrument is signed, numbered and dated by José, as well as being signed by Liam Romanillos.*

by Romanillos. Although the names of Bream and Romanillos still tend to be linked in much the same way as those of Segovia and Ramirez, Bream has in recent years shown an increased interest in the work of other luthiers.

By the early 1980s, Romanillos guitars had become much sought after by both performers and collectors, and this remains so to the present day. An admirer of both Torres and Hauser, Romanillos generally favours a pattern of seven fan struts – a Torres principle which was also adopted by Hauser. He is an outspoken critic of the acoustic properties of cedar, and known examples of Romanillos' work invariably have a spruce top. Since the mid 1970s, most Romanillos guitars have been built with Indian rosewood backs and sides, as in the example shown here, although a number of instruments, including one famous example owned by Bream, have been constructed using Brazilian rosewood.

Unconvinced by the potential benefits of extended string lengths, Romanillos builds instruments to the standard 650 mm unless the customer requests otherwise. A number of Romanillos guitars with a 645 mm string length are known to exist. Although he is sceptical

of the view that the choice of finish can profoundly affect the sound of the instrument, he is on record as advocating the use of French polish rather than the quicker and more modern methods adopted by many Spanish luthiers. A well-known feature of Romanillos guitars is the handmade rosette, which features an arch design inspired by the mosque at Córdoba.

In recent years, Romanillos has devoted much of his time to historical research. His definitive biography *Antonio de Torres, Guitar Maker – His Life & Work* was published in 1987, and his highly-acclaimed lectures on the life and career of Torres have featured at several international guitar festivals and summer schools. He is currently writing a book on the development of his own guitars, and a major historical survey of the Spanish guitar is nearing completion. Since the early 1990s, Romanillos has divided his time between England and Spain. His son Liam, who is a fully-trained craftsman in his own right, has become a partner in the business and now plays a major role in producing Romanillos guitars to his father's specification. ● PAUL FOWLES

▲ *The headstock of this Romanillos guitar is fitted with a set of engraved silver Landsdorfer machine heads that have mother-of-pearl buttons.*

all these respects, record companies are performing a service of incalculable value. A recording may not have the same resonances as a live performance, but it may well be the only performance you will hear in your lifetime.

The *Concierto de Aranjuez*, the most frequently played concerto in history, was never performed or recorded by Segovia, who was living in South America at the time of its first performance in Barcelona in 1940. The guitarist on that occasion was Regino Sainz de la Maza (1896-1981), who did not record it until 1968, by which time recordings had appeared by Narciso Yepes (1956), Julian Bream (1964), John Williams (1966), Alirio Díaz (1967) and some others. Since then, recordings have proliferated, some guitarists making up to three or four separate versions. Bream, Williams, Yepes, various Romeros, Parkening and Isbin and are some of those who have made recordings of this popular work, but so many versions are available at any given time, and doubtless more in the pipeline, that any specific recommendation would be out of date before it appeared in print. A full history of the work may be found in Graham Wade's 1985 book *Joaquín Rodrigo: Concierto de Aranjuez*, although the discography, inevitably, is in need of updating. Incidentally, Rodrigo wrote many other attractive pieces

composer, the profound nature of the work and the persuasive powers of Julian Bream, for whom it was written. Bream's intense performance has probably not been surpassed, but other guitarists have revealed the work's mysteries and wonders in their own way.

The music of Bach is a happy hunting ground for guitarists. A good introduction would be the two CDs of the so-called "lute" music performed with a luminous musicality by the Swedish guitarist Göran Söllscher. They feature a specially-made 11-string guitar that combines something of the facility of the baroque lute with the tonal qualities of a modern guitar.

Among contemporary composers, the Cuban Léo Brouwer (b.1939) has made a noteworthy contribution in the form of a continuous flow of composition, from the avant-garde to the neo-romantic and the minimalistic. *El Decameron Negro* (three episodes from African folklore) and *Paisaje Cubano con Campanas* ("Cuban Landscape with Bells") are fairly typical of his later writing. The first was written in 1981 for Sharon Isbin, who has recorded a perceptive performance of it. Good recordings of the latter are numerous, but a particularly well-played and well-recorded one is that made by Eduardo Isaacs, which was issued on the GHA label. Astor Piazzolla's modern tango-based compositions have also found a

◄ *No duo in guitar history has been more admired than that of Ida Presti (1924-1967) and Alexandre Lagoya (b.1929). Presti, who was French, started learning piano at five, then changed to the guitar, giving a recital in Paris at the age of ten. Lagoya was born in Egypt to Greek and Italian parents. He took up the guitar at eight, making his concert debut at 13. In 1951 they met in France and a year later they were married and began working as a duo. In the next 15 years they would play more than 2000 concerts. In 1967 Ida Presti was taken ill and died while they were in New York preparing for a concert. This 1963 record gives an idea of their range.*

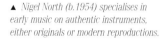

▲ *Nigel North (b.1954) specialises in early music on authentic instruments, either originals or modern reproductions.*

▲ *This 1990 album by Sharon Isbin (b.1956) reflects the eclecticism of young players today: from Tárrega to Jobim.*

▲ *Although he was only born in 1976, Slava Grigoryan is already an assured performer with a growing reputation. Born in Alma Ata, Kazakhstan, he emigrated to Australia with his family when he was five. His father, an orchestral violinist and composer, introduced him to the guitar. At eight he made his first public appearance: his first recital came at 14. In his final year at school he signed to Sony (formerly CBS), the first guitarist to join that label since another young Australian, John Williams. Like most young classical players he has wide-ranging tastes. This record celebrates Spain in repertoire largely familiar to Segovia, but it also includes pieces by jazz pianist Chick Corea. Similarly, his next disc, inspired by the tango tradition of Latin America, mixes Piazzolla and Baden Powell.*

for the guitar. *En los trigales*, *Invocación y danza*, and *Tres piezas españolas* are among those that come to mind.

The acute harmonic writing of Fernando Sor (1778-1839) has come to be admired more and more since the publication of his complete works by Tecla in the 1980s. *Variations on a theme of Mozart Op.9* has been much recorded, and two strong contenders must be Shin-ichi Fukuda and Nigel North, both playing period guitars. Other Sor works have come to the fore – *Fantaisie Elégiaque Op.59*, for instance, with its poignant funeral march.

The *Five Preludes* of Villa-Lobos (there are said to be six, but the sixth has never been traced) have also been much recorded. Bream, Santos, Yepes, Williams and Lagoya are among those who issued LPs. Segovia recorded only a couple of the Preludes, issued separately. Among very many more recent CD sets, those by Barrueco, Lieske, Kayath, Alexander-Sergei Ramirez and Tröster have much to offer, both in terms of recording and interpretation. Many of the foregoing have also recorded the *Twelve Studies*, to which might be added the name of Joaquim Freire. Some guitarists, like Frédéric Zigante, have recorded all Villa-Lobos's solo works. We may expect many more recordings of Villa-Lobos's small but seminal guitar *oeuvre*.

Britten's *Nocturnal after John Dowland Op.70* entered the repertoire in a very short time, helped by the name of a leading

place in the modern guitar repertoire. Aussel, Benitez, Pelech, Pierri, Söllscher, Tanenbaum and Tröster have all captured his unique vitality. In *Histoire du tango*, a duet in four episodes in varying styles from 1900 to the present day, the guitar is heard accompanying a variety of melodic instruments: flute, violin (perhaps the most idiomatic) and even the mandolin.

It would take a whole book to do justice to the abundant repertoire and the very large number of recordings issued. Many of them go virtually unnoticed. Even the 178 pages of the British monthly music magazine *Gramophone* can accommodate no more than two or three guitar reviews. The specialist magazine *Classical Guitar* publishes on average 15 guitar record reviews every month, and even that represents rather less than a quarter of the total number of records submitted for review.

The future, as always, is unclear. We can expect more versions of the *Concierto de Aranjuez*. There will be more exploration of Sor and Giuliani, probably on period instruments. Good contemporary guitar music will be recorded along with the bad, as it usually is. Russia and China may produce virtuosos who will record in editions running into millions. The guitar will blossom as an ensemble instrument, particularly in voice accompaniment, for which it is well suited. But prophets are usually proved wrong. The golden age of guitar recording could well be here and now. ● **COLIN COOPER**

GUITAR MUSIC: CLASSICAL CROSSOVER

During the first half of the 20th century, the gut-string predecessor of the modern nylon-string guitar was rarely heard outside classical music and the folk music of Spain and Latin America. The steel-string plectrum guitar, meanwhile, had reached a position where it had become increasingly common in the mainstream popular music of Europe and of North America.

By the 1940s, it had replaced the banjo in the rhythm sections of dance bands, and such pioneering figures as Charlie Christian and Eddie Lang had become familiar to the attention of the record-buying public. Elsewhere, the guitar was gaining ground as a featured solo instrument, the early recordings of the Quintette du Hot Club de France showing that the guitar of Django Reinhardt was more than a match for the violin virtuosity of Stephane Grappelli.

In the 1950s, however, things changed. The arrival of bossa nova from Brazil, with nylon-string guitar as the central instrument, soon attracted jazz musicians in North America, and a generation of Brazilian guitarists suddenly found themselves on the world stage.

The first to achieve international fame was Laurindo Almeida (1917-95). A Brazilian classical guitarist who took up jazz after seeing Reinhardt, Almeida had moved to the US in 1947, becoming

developed his guitar skills in Greenwich Village coffee shops, José Feliciano (b.1945) achieved international success with his laidback account of 'California Dreamin'' and a bossa nova reworking of The Doors' 'Light My Fire'. The latter features one of the most concise and brilliant acoustic guitar breaks ever to appear on a three-minute single. Feliciano combined flamenco right-hand techniques with the rhythmic and melodic ideas of rock, blues and Latin jazz. Apart from a wide range of vocal numbers (including the two hit singles) his 1968 LP *Feliciano!* contains dazzling instrumental settings of The Beatles' 'And I Love Her' and 'Here, There and Everywhere'.

In the same year, the American singer and guitarist Mason Williams enjoyed overnight success with his instrumental composition 'Classical Gas'. Although Williams went on to record the piece on solo guitar, the single version was augmented by a powerful Mike Post orchestration. Ironically both versions were played on a metal-string guitar, but the success of 'Classical Gas' encouraged recognition of the "classical" side of the instrument.

One of many guitarists to have released a cover version of 'Classical Gas' is the veteran "country picker" Chet Atkins (b.1924). As head of RCA Nashville, Atkins launched the careers of numerous country and western stars and was a key figure in the development

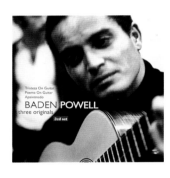

▲ Charlie Byrd (b.1925) is rare in earning his living inside the world of jazz while playing a nylon-strung guitar. He was taught the basics at seven, by his father, and, like Julian Bream, did his military service as a guitarist in a dance band run by the army. But after World War II he was also smitten with the classical guitar, studying seriously with Sophocles Papas and then briefly with Segovia. Thereafter, he returned to jazz, leading his own trio, playing in Woody Herman's big band, still on nylon strings, and touring the world. In South America he encountered the bossa nova, which he popularised with Stan Getz. This 1996 compilation shows his sheer range.

▲ The Brazilian guitarist Laurindo Almeida (1917-1955) recorded these Latin jazz tracks in 1958 with saxman Bud Shank.

▲ The bossa nova and samba playing of Baden Powell de Aquino (b.1937) has influenced guitarists from many schools.

▲ This 1973 double-album by rock group Yes included on side three a nylon-string guitar solo by Steve Howe (b.1947).

▲ Incantation rode the mid-1980s craze for Andean music. Their guitarist Forbes Henderson (b.1951) is a classical player.

guitarist with the Stan Kenton orchestra. After leaving Kenton, in 1950, Almeida concentrated on session work, and it was during this period that he produced a number of acclaimed classical recordings.

But he also began to perform Brazilian material with his own trio, and in 1953 worked with saxophonist Bud Shank on a couple of records that either anticipated bossa nova or influenced its development. It was this early-1960s global craze that made Laurindo Almeida one of the most influential guitarists of his time. An early convert was an American, Charlie Byrd (b.1925), who had been playing nylon-string guitar in jazz as well as working on his classical playing. He soon acquired the Latin sound, joining saxman Stan Getz for the 1962 LP *Jazz Samba*, a huge international hit.

By the mid-1960s, more Brazilian guitarists were making their mark on the North American jazz scene. Foremost among these was Baden Powell (b.1937) who arrived in New York during the summer of 1966 at the invitation of Getz. Powell went on to make such historic solo recordings as *Tristeza On Guitar* and *Poema On Guitar*, both of which were well received by the European market.

With the nylon-string guitar firmly established as a force in jazz, the scene was set for its arrival in the world of popular music. Fittingly, the first two hit singles to feature the instrument in anything more than a supporting role came from a guitarist of Puerto Rican origin. A blind singer and songwriter who had

of the "Nashville Sound". He was also a long-time exponent of the nylon-string guitar, and his awareness of the technical problems of amplifying the instrument led to the innovative Gibson Chet Atkins model. A solidbody electric guitar with nylon strings and a classical-type neck and headstock, this curious hybrid allows the player unlimited dynamic control but inevitably lacks the natural resonance of a conventional acoustic instrument.

The early 1970s was the heyday of what the English disc-jockey John Peel later dubbed "art rock". For the first time in the history of rock music it was considered desirable to be "classically trained", although few, if any, of the guitar heroes of the period could claim an academic background in any formal sense. However, this was the period in which the classical voice of the guitar finally made its debut in the world of popular music.

Heavy metal bands such as Black Sabbath would enhance the gothic atmosphere of their recordings by including classically-inspired "bridges" between album tracks. Steve Howe's gentle and contemplative 'Mood For A Day' became the piece every aspiring guitarist would learn, having mastered the opening of 'Stairway To Heaven'. Mike Oldfield's epic *Tubular Bells* allowed the classical guitar the final word in the closing moments of side one, and Steve Hackett of Genesis opened side two of *Foxtrot* with the quasi-baroque 'Horizons'. A few years later, in 1977, the title track of *A*

Farewell To Kings by the Canadian band Rush featured a "classical" prelude and reprise performed by lead guitarist Alex Lifeson.

One guitarist who took the concept further than any other at the time was Jan Akkerman. An award-winning rock guitarist with jazz leanings, Akkerman was a member of the Dutch band Focus. The 1971 *Moving Waves* featured 'Le Clochard', an Akkerman composition for classical guitar and Mellotron strings, and the subsequent *Focus 3* and *Hamburger Concerto* albums found Akkerman performing on both classical guitar and Renaissance lute. Akkerman's solo releases explored the territory further still, the 1974 album *Tabernakel* featuring authentic 16th century lute solos alongside a new electric guitar arrangement of 'House Of The King' (an Akkerman composition from the first Focus album) and the ethereal 'Javeh' for classical guitar and orchestra.

In the same period, classical guitarist John Williams (b.1941) was taking his first steps toward the world of popular music. His recording of Stanley Myers' 'Cavatina' (later used in the 1978 movie *The Deer Hunter*) was released as a single in 1971, and the accompanying album *Changes* contained an experimental rock-based setting of the *Prelude* from J.S. Bach's *Suite in E major*. The 1973 album *The Height Below*, which was Williams' first

Meeting Of The Spirits. Lucia's association with McLaughlin has continued through the 1980s and 1990s, their most recent recording being *The Guitar Trio*, in which the third guitarist is Al di Meola, formerly a member of Chick Corea's Return To Forever.

In Britain, the London-based flamenco guitarist Juan Martin (b.1943) entered the UK singles chart in 1983 with the romantic and decidedly non-flamenco 'Love Theme from The Thorn Birds' - a Henry Mancini composition for a TV movie set in Australia. Martin is an inspired and original musician who, like Paco de Lucia, often incurs the wrath of flamenco purists. His subsequent projects have included a set of compositions inspired by the paintings of Picasso and a concert tour with the tabla player Chris Karan.

One group whose work is notoriously difficult to categorise is The Gipsy Kings. Characterised by a gruff yet expressive vocal style and the exuberant strumming of flamenco guitars, The Gipsy Kings successfully captured the public imagination during the 1980s and remain a popular attraction to this day. Their most famous song 'Bamboleo' is still often heard on UK radio, a rare achievement in a country notoriously resistant to records sung in a foreign language.

Since the late 1980s, the highly-acclaimed Cuban classical guitarist Manuel Barrueco (b.1952) has shown considerable interest

▲ *This 1971 album, the start of John Williams' interest in pop music, mixes Bach with The Beatles and Joni Mitchell.*

▲ *Alexandre Lagoya joined the French jazz pianist Claude Bolling for this 1982 account of the latter's concerto.*

▲ *Al DiMeola (b.1954), John McLaughlin (b.1942) and Paco De Lucia (b.1947) combine Latin, jazz-rock and flamenco.*

▲ *A 1993 album by The Gipsy Kings, a pop sensation created by two sets of brothers from strong flamenco backgrounds.*

collaboration with the composer Brian Gascoigne, is considered by many to be the most successful of all his away fixtures.

Performing on classical and electric guitars, Williams entered the realms of jazz and Eastern folk music with the support of an Indian percussionist, a Japanese koto player and a team of London session musicians. To the disappointment of enthusiasts, *The Height Below* had no direct sequel. But it led indirectly to the late-1970s formation of Sky, a classical rock ensemble which, despite an all-star line-up, yielded little of lasting value. Nonetheless, the huge popularity of Sky greatly increased public awareness of the classical guitar.

One of the most outstanding crossover works of the 1970s was the *Concerto for Classical Guitar and Jazz Piano* by the French composer Claude Bolling (b.1930). Originally in six movements, this brilliant and inventive work was later augmented by a spectacular Finale inspired by the classical guitar virtuosity of Angel Romero. After performing the work alongside the composer at the Hollywood Bowl in 1979, Romero went on to record it in 1980 with George Shearing (piano), Ray Brown (bass) and Shelly Manne (drums).

From the 1970s onwards, flamenco guitarists have shown an increasing inclination to explore beyond their home territory. One of the central figures in this development has been Paco de Lucia (b.1947) whose 1979 collaboration with jazz-rock guitarists John McLaughlin and Larry Coryell resulted in the pace-setting live album

in jazz and popular music. His 1994 recording *Sometime Ago* contained a stylish and idiomatic account of Keith Jarrett's 'Köln Concert Part IIc', and his next release featured Beatles songs arranged for guitar and orchestra by his compatriot Leo Brouwer.

Soon after this, two guitar recordings emerged which effectively completed the cross-pollination of popular and classical music. In 1996, the German classical guitarists Thomas Offermann and Jens Wagner, collectively known as Duo Sonare, released a groundbreaking arrangement for two guitars of the entire content of Mike Oldfield's *Tubular Bells*. As well as being a technical tour de force, this incredible performance displays a complete understanding of Oldfield's musical language.

Less than a year later, Steve Hackett confounded his critics by entering the HMV classical chart with his orchestral fantasia *A Midsummer Night's Dream*. Performing with the Royal Philharmonic Orchestra, he emerges as a fully-fledged classical guitarist and composer. *A Midsummer Night's Dream* can accurately be described as a substantial contemporary work.

So, as we approach the millennium, two leading classical guitarists are reviving one of the rock masterpieces of the 1970s, and a leading exponent of 1970s rock is performing his own compositions with a major British orchestra. Whatever would Segovia have said? ● PAUL FOWLES

▲ *The British performer Sting has long been fascinated by Latin American rhythms and sounds. This 1993 album, like all his records since 1991's The Soul Cages, features guitarist Dominic Miller (b.1961), who was brought up in Buenos Aires, Argentina. Miller is principally a nylon-string player, who spent a year studying classical guitar at the Guildhall in London before leaving to play electric guitar in various bands. But it was session work playing nylon-strung guitar, notably on Phil Collins's But Seriously... album, that led him to Sting. Miller played his Miguel Rodríguez classical on The Soul Cages, but increasingly he uses an electric classical called a P-Project.*

GLOSSARY

Action Height of strings above fingerboard.

Alerce South American tree related to the larch.

Alphabeto A 17th century Italian notation system using an alphabet of chord symbols.

Apoyando A right-hand technique also known as the rest stroke, in which the playing finger passes 'through' the string, coming to rest on the adjacent string.

Arched Term used to describe a soundboard that curves across the body of the guitar

Arpeggio A broken chord, in which the notes are played sequentially rather than together.

Arrangement Adaptation of music intended for other instruments to the guitar. Also the music that emerges at the end of the process.

Atonal A type of composition, usually of the 20th century, which has no allegiance to a tonal centre.

Bandurría Spanish folk instrument with a pear-shaped body and steel strings.

Belly Soundboard of the guitar.

Binding A continuous strip of wood fitted to the outer edge of a guitar body for decorative purposes.

Bookmatched Made from a piece of wood split into two sheets and joined with the grain matching symmetrically.

Bordón or **Bourdon** Lowest string on an early guitar.

Bossa nova A musical style derived from the influence of West Coast jazz upon Brazilian samba rhythms.

Bout Upper or lower section of the guitar body.

Braces Wood structures beneath guitar front and back intended to enhance strength and tonal response.

Bracing The pattern of braces used in a guitar.

Brazilian rosewood Hardwood derived from the tropical evergreen *Dalbergia nigra* and used in the making of guitar bodies. Now a protected species, meaning further exportation from Brazil is banned.

Bridge Rectangular block of wood to which strings are attached, usually by tying.

Bridge-block The drilled section through which the strings are threaded.

Bridge plate Flat plate on soundboard beneath bridge, favoured by some builders who make it part of their strutting pattern.

Button Knob used to turn machine heads.

Café cantante Flamenco café in 19th century Spain.

Cante Song: one of the components of flamenco.

Capo (capo tasto, capo dastro) A movable device for clamping the strings at a particular fret to raise the guitar's pitch.

Cedar Evergreen conifer of the Mediterranean, used particularly in the making of necks. Not to be confused with 'western red cedar', which is not a cedar at all but a North American *thuya* or arbor vitae.

Chitarra battente Steel-strung guitar used in the popular music of 18th century Italy.

Cittern Small flat pear-shaped instrument with metal strings, popular in Europe from the middle ages to the 18th century. Not to be confused with the gittern.

Compás The rhythmic pattern of a flamenco piece.

Concert guitar Guitar intended for the public performance of 'serious' music.

Concerto An extended work for a solo instrument and an orchestra.

Continuo Music improvised over a written bassline.

Counterpoint Music made up of two or more independent melody lines.

Coupling Exchange of mechanical energy between string and soundboard.

Course A pair of strings tuned in unison or an octave apart, as used in Baroque guitars.

Cuadro A flamenco group.

Cypress A conifer native to Southern Europe, East Asia and North America and widely planted for decorative purposes and for timber. Used in the 19th century for the bodies of cheaper guitars and taken up by the flamencos.

Dissonance Clash between two notes sounded together.

Domed Used of a soundboard that is arched both longitudinally and transversely.

End-block Thick wooden block used to join sides of guitar at the lower bout.

English guitar An 18th century version of the cittern.

Etude or **Study** Piece intended to help players develop their technical skills, sometimes also of musical value.

European spruce Sometimes called German spruce, *picea abies* tends to come from the Balkans. Spruce originally meant "from Prussia". Used for soundboards.

F-hole Soundhole in approximate f-shape, usually on "jazz" archtop guitars.

Falseta Set of guitar variations in flamenco.

Fan-strutting Wooden struts beneath lower soundboard of guitar, arranged in approximately the shape of an open fan.

Fantasia (16th century) contrapuntal piece; (19th century) poetic, allusive piece with no fixed form.

Fingerboard The surface, often of ebony, glued to the neck to carrry the frets.

Flamenca negra Flamenco guitar in rosewood rather than cypress.

Flamenco Andalusian music and dance form, showing Gypsy and Moorish inheritance; person who plays flamenco music.

Foot Part of the neck which extends inside the body.

French polishing A traditional varnishing technique that uses a small fabric pad to rub shellac dissolved in alcohol into the wood of a guitar body.

Fret Metal strip across fingerboard used to determine pitch. Ivory or gut were used on early instruments.

Fretboard The fingerboard.

Friction peg Traditional tuning peg held in position by friction of wood in hole. Now only on flamenco guitars.

Gittern Small gut-strung lute of the Renaissance era, formerly considered an ancestor of the guitar.

Glue-blocks Small wooden blocks used to glue top and back of guitar to sides.

Golpeador Thin protective plate used to protect the tops of flamenco guitars against finger-tapping.

Guitarrero Guitar maker.

Guitarrista Guitarist.

Gumi-laca Spanish name for the natural lacquer used in French polishing.

Gut Cured animal intestines used for strings before development of nylon.

Harmonic bar Reinforcing bar glued to the inside of the soundboard across the body of the guitar.

Harmonics Overtones, or higher frequency sounds generated at the same time as any fundamental note; a technique involving sounding those higher frequency notes by touching the string to damp the fundamental.

Head Extension of the neck, holding tuners.

Heel Part of the neck block to which the sides are fitted and which remains outside the body.

Indian rosewood Hardwood from a tropical evergreen tree known as East Indian rosewood or *Dalbergia latifolia*. Used in making guitar bodies, especially now Brazilian rosewood is not freely available.

Juerga Spontaneous flamenco event.

Kerfed lining A lining that has been partly cut through at intervals to make it flexible enough to follow the shape of the guitar's sides.

Lacquer A traditional finish for guitars, usually hand-applied over a long period.

Laud Small Spanish folk instrument with metal strings.

Legato Smoothly.

Ligado Left-hand technique involving hammering on and pulling off. Especially important in flamenco.

Lining A continuous strip of wood used to join sides to top and back.

Lower bout Section of guitar body below waist.

Lute Medieval and renaissance musical instrument.

Luthier Guitar maker.

Machine heads Mechanical gears for altering string tension and pitch.

Modes of vibration The different types of vibration in any vibrating body.

Mother-of-pearl Shell of some molluscs, used for decoration of rosettes, tuning pegs etc.

Neck-block The end of the neck as it meets the body, built up to join to sides, top and back.

Nocturne A piece relating to night and its associations.

Nodal bar In some guitars by David Rubio, a strut extending from beneath the bridge on the treble side of the soundboard. Intended to modify treble response.

Node A stationary part of a vibrating body.

Nut Bar of ivory or bone determining string spacing and height at head end of neck.

Picado In flamenco, a fast run picked out with two fingers of the right hand.

Pin bridge A bridge that secures the strings by pins rather than by tying.

Pitch Frequency of a note.

Plantilla The outline of a guitar body.

Plate Scientific term for the vibrating soundboard.

Plectrum Object held in right hand to strike strings.

Polyphonic Music made up of several independent lines, known as voices.

Prelude Originally the opening piece of a set. But since the 19th century, preludes no longer have to precede.

Punteado The plucking of individual notes.

Purfling Decorative inlays around the perimeter of the guitar alongside the binding.

Quarter-sawn Wood cut on radius of tree so that rings are perpendicular to the surface of the plank.

Rasguedo Strumming.

Re-entrant tuning Type of tuning in which strings are not arranged in order of pitch across the neck.

Resonant frequency The frequency at which any object is likely to vibrate most with the least stimulation.

Ribs The sides of the guitar.

Rib-block Wooden block used to support harmonic and transverse bars.

Rose Intricate fretted wood or parchment covering for soundhole in early guitars.

Rosette Intricate decoration around soundhole, usually in marquetry or wood mosaic.

Saddle Strip of bone or ivory that the strings pass over at the bridge.

Samba Brazilian dance with African origins.

Scale length The distance from nut to twelfth fret multiplied by two.

Shellac A natural thermoplastic resin made from the secretions of the lac insect, which lives on trees in India and Thailand. Dissolved in alcohol to create a finish that is applied to guitars by French polishing.

Sitka spruce or *Picea sitchensis*, a large conifer, originally from North America. Used for soundboards, especially by US makers.

Soundboard The vibrating top of a guitar body.

Soundhole Hole in body to facilitate sound projection.

Splice-joint One method of fixing head to neck.

Spruce A coniferous tree, also known as the "Spruce-fir", found throughout the Northern hemisphere.

String length Sounding length of string, measured from nut to bridge saddle.

String-block The drilled section of a bridge through which the strings are threaded.

Struts Wood structures beneath guitar front and back to enhance strength and tonal response.

Strutting The pattern of struts used.

Study or *Etude* Piece intended for pedagogic purposes, sometimes also of musical value.

Suite A group of pieces based on dance forms.

Sympathetic resonances Sound produced by open strings that are not struck.

Syncopation Displacement of the normal beat.

Tablao Stage, or flamenco night-club.

Tablature System of musical notation indicating the position of the fingers on frets and strings.

Table The soundboard or top of a guitar.

Tango Argentinian dance related to the Cuban habañera and probably of African origin; also flamenco dance, said to be of Arabic origin.

Tapa Spanish word for soundboard. Literally 'the lid'.

Theorbo A type of large lute.

Thicknessing The process of shaving and sanding guitar parts to the required thickness.

Timbre Tone quality.

Tirando Right hand technique also known as the free stroke, in which the playing finger plucks the string but does not make contact with the adjacent string.

Tonewood Wood used in the making of musical instruments.

Top The soundboard, also known as the table.

Toque Flamenco guitar playing.

Tornavoz Metal cylinder inside soundhole intended to aid projection. Used by Torres but now scorned.

Transcription The adaptation of music intended for other instruments to the guitar; also the piece of music that emerges from the process.

Transverse bar Bar glued across back of guitar.

Tuning pegs Machine heads or friction pegs.

'Ud Arabic instrument introduced into Spain by the Moors, with important consequences for lute making.

Upper bout Section of guitar body above waist.

V-joint One method of fixing head to neck or neck to body. More complex than normal splice-joint.

Variations Embellishments of a musical theme.

Varnish Protective and decorative surface applied to guitar bodies. Ranges from shellac applied by French polishing to man-made urethane applied by spray.

Vihuela Spanish instrument of the 15th and 16th centuries, resembling the guitar in appearance but musically closer to the lute.

Vihuela de mano Plucked version of the vihuela

Virtuoso An instrumental performer with excellent technical abilities.

Waist Narrowest part of guitar body.

Waisted Guitar body with figure-of-eight shape.

Western red cedar Not a cedar at all but *Thuya plicata*, the North American arbor vitae, a conifer that can grow to 40 m. Introduced as a soundboard material by José Ramírez III and now used by many makers.

Wolf note On stringed instruments, a note with a sound unpleasantly different from those around it. This phenomenon is much affected by guitar construction.

INDEX

*Page numbers in italics refer
to illustrations*